MARCO

W9-CQF-289

Travel with
Insider
Tips

FINLAND

SWEDEN

FINLAND

NORWAY

RUSSIA

Helsinki

Oslo Stockholm

Saint
Petersburg

ESTONIA

LATVIA

Moscow

LITHUANIA
RUS BELARUS
POLAND

www.marcopolouk.com

SYMBOLS

INSIDER TIP   Insider Tip

★   Highlight

●●●●   Best of ...

🔆   Scenic view

🍃   Responsible travel: for ecological or fair trade aspects

(*)   Telephone numbers that
are not toll-free

PRICE CATEGORIES
HOTELS

Expensive   over 150 euros

Moderate   75–150 euros

Budget   under 75 euros

Price for a double room,
with breakfast

PRICE CATEGORIES
RESTAURANTS

Expensive   over 25 euros

Moderate   15–25 euros

Budget   under 15 euros

Prices based on an average
meal without drinks

On the cover: Saimaa – lakes as far as the eye can see p. 69 | Sweating it out p. 78

CONTENTS

Finnish lake district p. 64

East Finland → p. 80

Lapland → p. 88

Road atlas → p. 122

DID YOU KNOW?
Timeline → p. 12
Local specialities → p. 26
Books & films → p. 43
Budgeting → p. 111
Currency converter → p. 113
Weather in Helsinki → p. 115

MAPS IN THE GUIDEBOOK
(124 A1) Page numbers
and coordinates refer to
the road atlas
(O) Site/address located off
the map. Coordinates are
also given for places that are
not marked on the road atlas
(U A1) Refers to the Helsinki
street map inside the back
cover

INSIDE BACK COVER:
PULL-OUT MAP →

PULL-OUT MAP 🗺
(🗺 A–B 2–3) Refers to the
removable pull-out map
(🗺 a–b 2–3) Refers to the
additional insert map on
the pull-out map

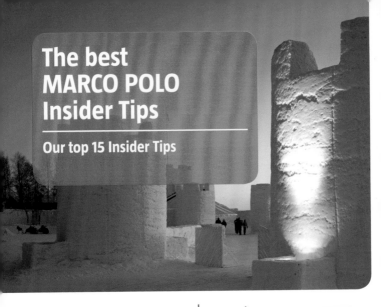

The best MARCO POLO Insider Tips

Our top 15 Insider Tips

BEST OF ...

FOR FREE

● *Fantastic architecture for free*
Entrance to Helsinki's 'Rock Church' is always free except when there is a concert. With a bit of luck you might be there for a rehearsal and can listen to a concert for free, too → p. 35

● *Skerry hopping for nothing*
All yellow ferries in the skerries off Turku can be used without charge; cyclists and pedestrians can also travel free on some of the white ferries. Enjoy the special atmosphere of the islands and the lovely west coast → p. 56

● *Off for a swim*
Access to beaches on the west coast is free for everyone. You can sunbathe or go swimming wherever you want. The beaches in Kalajoki are especially big → p. 57

● *A marvellous concert hall*
The Sibelius Hall in Lahti is one of the most beautiful in Finland and can be visited free of charge when there are no performances → p. 45

● *A Garden of Eden*
The beautiful Hätänpää Arboretum (photo) in Tampere is an oasis of peace and quiet. You can take a look at the sea of flowers in the 27-acre botanical garden with its 500 species of plant free of charge. The arboretum is especially lovely in late summer when the rose garden is at its best → p. 76

● *Three museums for free*
Entrance to museums in Jyväskylä on Fridays is free, whether it's the Alvar Aalto Museum, the Craft Museum or the Art Museum and Centre for Printmaking → p. 76

● *Free accommodation in the middle of nowhere*
Access to all national parks is free. And you can even stay the night in several cabins in the wilderness – in Pallas Yllästunturi National Park, for instance – for nothing, but you'll need to be properly equipped → p. 92

●●●● Dots in guidebook refer to 'Best of ...' tips

ONLY IN FINLAND
Unique experiences

● *Celebrate midsummer*
On the weekend after midsummer's day, Finland celebrates the never-ending days of summer. Join in: decorate a traditional 'St John's tree' in Mariehamn open-air museum or witness the biggest midsummer bonfire on Seurasaari in Helsinki → p. 36, 53

● *Singing is good for you!*
Karaoke bars are popular among singing-loving Finns. Have a drink before plucking up courage and singing your heart out! Or book the coolest 'music room' in Helsinki – the karaoke taxi → p. 43

● *Breaking into a sweat*
Finland is sauna-land. The best way to experience this is in your own summerhouse on a lake. Or visit the Sauna Museum in Muurame and find out about the very first type of sweatbox – the smoke sauna → p. 67

● *Tracing Kalevala back to its roots*
The Finnish national epic, *Kalevala*, is written in verse. In the runic singers' village Ilomantsi you can find out about Karelian culture and listen to the *kantele*, the Finnish zither → p. 83

● *Take a walk on the wild side*
The majority of Finland is covered by forests and lakes, and marked by glacial formations. The hiking regions are correspondingly huge and untouched. The most famous wilderness in Finland is the Oulanka National Park → p. 86

● *In a one-deer open sleigh*
It's a truly unqiue experience being pulled through the deep snow in Lapland by a reindeer or a pack of huskies. And there's no better way to get a feeling for the vastness of the Finnish winter – for example near Muonio → p. 103

● *Feeling the pulse of the Finns: the tango*
Finland is tango country – danced in the melancholic and pensive way. But nobody's singing the blues here. Quite the contrary: tango is an attitude – and, once a year, little Seinäjoki is turned into a place of pilgrimage for tango aficionados (photo) → p. 107

ONLY IN

BEST OF ...

● *A shopping spree without getting wet feet*
Finnish brand names under one roof: in places like Stockmann, Helsinki's largest department store (photo) or in the biggest 'village shop' in the country (near Ähtäri), you may well hope that it rains a little bit longer → p. 28, 40

● *Coffee to stay*
A rainy morning soon passes by at the breakfast buffet in the time-honoured Café Ekberg in Helsinki → p. 39

● *Try your hand*
At the craft museum in Turku anything's possible: you can become a goldsmith, furrier, weaver, baker or blacksmith for a day → p. 61

● *Off to the paper museum*
The historic white board mill in Verla is a Unesco World Heritage Site. Guided tours take you on a journey to the origins of the Finnish paper industry. If you want to, you can also stay the night on the museum site in former workers' cottages → p. 71

● *Immerse yourself in Finnish music*
The spectrum of music in Finland is huge. One rainy afternoon alone will not be enough to get the full picture. As in all larger libraries, the music department in the Metso Library in Tampere will make a compilation of Finnish CDs for you covering all types of music which you can listen to in a music room → p. 76

● *Time to experiment*
When the weather is bad, the Heureka science centre in Vantaa can brighten up the day and provide a lot of fun with experiments full of surprises and masses of different ways of seeing what it is like to be a boffin → p. 104

RAIN

RELAX AND CHILL OUT
Take it easy and spoil yourself

● *Bathing in privacy*

The red cliffs of the Åland Islands are ideal for sunbathing: beautifully warm and smooth. A floating sauna boat complete with captain will take you to your very own private bay → **p. 55**

● *Beach spa*

How about a swim out to sea or would you prefer a massage instead? Or simply indulge in one after the after? In the tropical Eden Holiday Club on Oulu beach you can be pampered however you like and let the day draw to a close with a long walk along the beach → **p. 60**

● *Pure indulgence*

Have you ever dreamt of a wooden cabin on a lake but with all the creature comforts of a luxury hotel? If you're hankering after such a combination, you'll love the Anttolanhovi spa resort in the Saimaa lake district. There are generously-sized houses and comfortable rooms, a spa with a turf sauna, honey baths and lots of fresh sea air → **p. 71**

● *The good old days*

Tuck into Finnish specialities and enjoy the sun on deck while gliding through the beautiful lakeland scenery and past dense forests on a nostalgic boat trip aboard the old *M/S Pujo* from Savonlinna to Kuopio → **p. 73**

● *Limb alignment*

In the Frantsila Herb Farm spa near Hämeenkyrö everything revolves around your well-being. Reiki, a herbal sauna and Ayurveda are all on the agenda. After a traditional Finnish 'limb alignment' session at the latest, your body and soul will be in perfect harmony → **p. 79**

● *Under the Northern Lights*

In the Arktikum in Rovaniemi (photo) you can lie comfortably on your back while the Northern Lights and mystic tales glide past your eyes on a huge sky-like screen → **p. 92**

INTRODUCTION

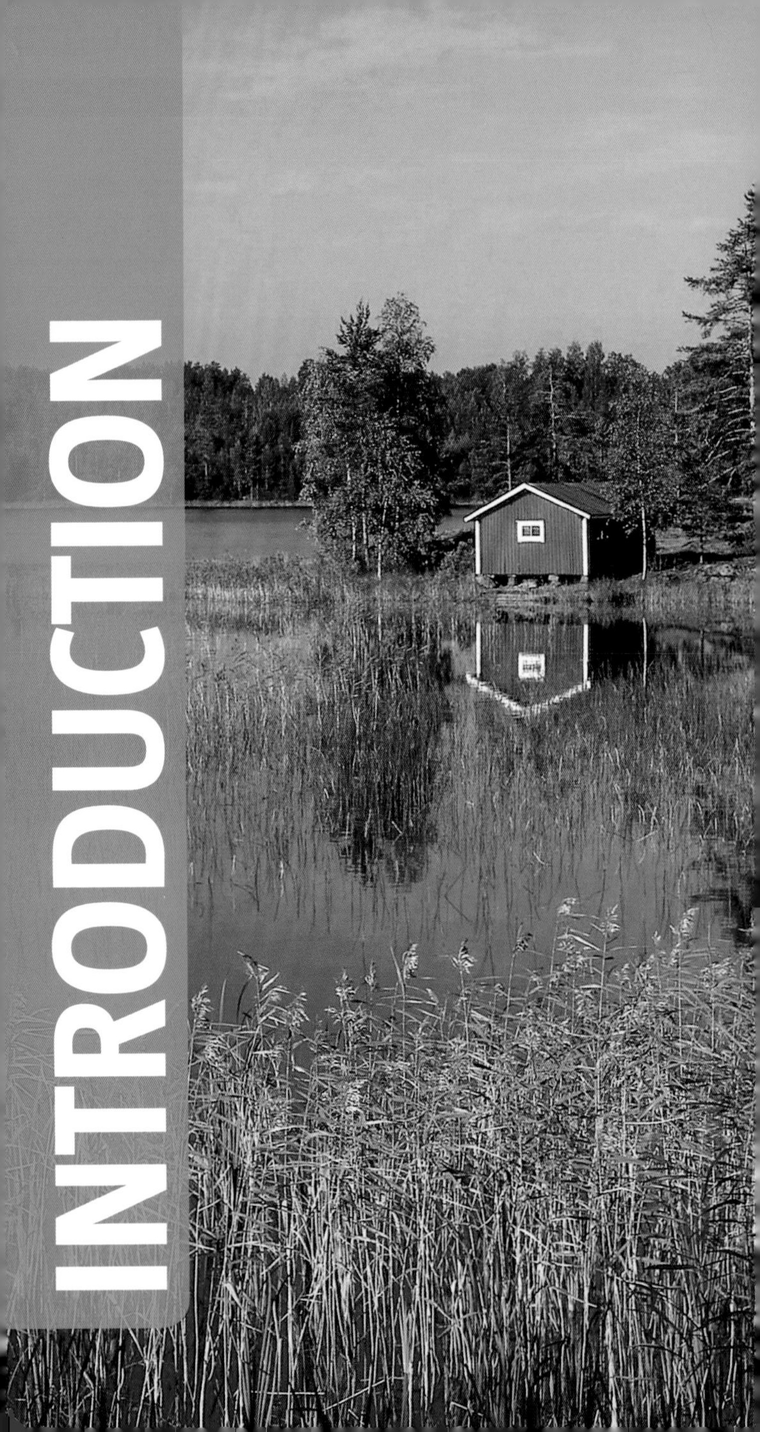

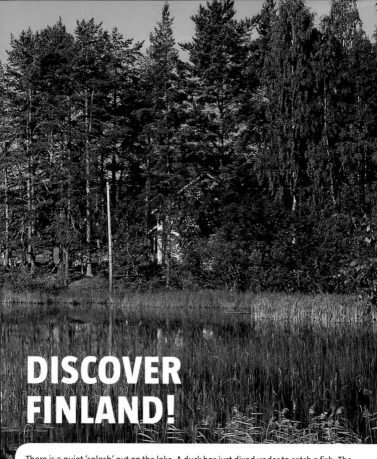

DISCOVER FINLAND!

There is a quiet 'splash' out on the lake. A duck has just dived under to catch a fish. The concentric circles on the glassy surface of the water show where the bird disappeared from view. Somewhere in the forest around about, the tell-tale tapping of a wood-pecker can be heard. Otherwise there is nothing. Only peace and quiet, the little cabin on the lake, the jetty and the sun that is high in the sky. *Tervetuloa Suomeen* – Welcome to Finland! Welcome to the far north, to the wild and lonely part of Europe.

Finland is often called the 'country of thousands of lakes' – but this is a slight under-statement. Anyone who comes here can look forward to some 200,000 lakes, 2 million saunas and sheer endless forests. The countryside is like a flecked carpet of blues and greens with a scattering of little red-painted houses with white windows in between. These Bullerby-like log cabins with saunas, called *mökki* in Finnish, are a paradise for nature-lovers. No rushing around, no stess, no noise: two weeks at the lakeside are pure balsam for the soul. And whoever needs a change of scenery between whiles drops in on the neighbours – the Finns really know how to enjoy the summer.

Photo: Sauna cabin in the Saimaa lake district

The cathedral in Helsinki welcomes those who arrive by sea

Only 5.3 million people live in *Suomi*, as the Finnish call their country. Their way of living is governed by the short summer when everything comes to life with a rush. Anybody travelling around the country in mid summer – around 21 June – will find that nobody goes to sleep: they are all out celebrating. In summer, life shifts to the countryside; out of the cities and into the great outdoors. The sun never sets, but bathes the night in a diffuse, silvery dusk-like light. These are carefree days when life is celebrated to the full, such as during the lively festivities around Midsummer's Day or tango dancing under a starry sky. The largest tango festival of its kind takes place every year in July in a little place called Seinäjoki. And with the summer, a range of weird and wonderful competitions takes place, such as motocross races on dirt tracks, swamp soccer, boat races, or wellie-throwing competitions – a sport that is already well-established in

In summer everything bursts into life

98 AD
First mention of the 'Fenni' people by Tacitus in *Germania*

1550
First settlement in Helsinki

1700–1721
In the Great Northern War, Sweden loses control of the region and Karelia falls to Russia

1809
Sweden concedes Finland to the Tsardom of Russia

1812
Helsinki becomes the capital

1835
Elias Lönnrot publishes the Finnish national epic, *Kalevala*

England. But as strange as these events may seem, they are also rather deceptive. The Finns are not cultural 'lightweights'. Quite the opposite. The summer is also a time for established cultural highlights. In Savonlinna, the Covent Garden of the north, the world-famous opera festival is held every year in July. And high-calibre art finds its way beyond the very last birch tree: internationally well-known artists tour the country from June until August, playing at the chamber music festival in Kuhmo on the Russian border, for example, or attending the Midnight Sun Film Festival in tiny Sodankylä in Lappland. There is always enough space for theatrical performances in summer, even in the smallest of villages. And you may even be surprised to find works of art right in the middle of nowhere.

The most important ingredient for a perfect summer, however, is that little holiday house called a *mökki*. Vitually every Finn has one – or at least has friends who own one. While Helsinki is left to the tourists

> **A house on a lake and the holiday is perfect**

in the summer – and several pubs and restaurants in the capital are closed between June and August – the locals relax in their cabins and recover from a year of hard work, the city, the noise and the adversities of life. Every *mökki* has a sauna – something that can be taken for granted in just the same way as every *mökki* has a front door and windows. And should you ever be invited by friends or neighbours to join them for a sauna during their holiday, don't turn it down whatever you do: an invitation to a sauna is the Finnish token of friendship *per se*.

The comforting heat of the sauna also helps the Finns through the long winter months, when the arctic darkness falls across the country. Traditional Finns brave the cold and go off on cross-country skis or snoeshoes to keep fit – virtually every town and village has floodlit cross-country tracks and trails. Modern-thinking northerners prefer to zoom around on snowmobiles, roaring at up to 70 km/h through the snowy country-side. Whatever your preference, a sauna afterwards is a must – and the really hardy types cool off afterwards by jumping through a hole in the ice! Everyone goes to great pains to make life in the dark and cold as varied as possible and to carry on as usual despite adverse conditions. The Finns face up to the forces of Nature with a doggedness typical of the country as a whole. Airports, for example, operate normally even in extreme conditions and mountains of snow are removed as a matter of course.

1863	1906	1917	1918	1919
Finnish becomes the second official language after Swedish	Finland is the first European country to introduce women's suffrage	Parliament declares the independence of the State of Finland on 6 December	Civil war breaks out during the secession from Russia. The Communists are defeated by democratic forces	Founding of the Republic of Finland; peace treaty and border agreement with Soviet Russia one year later

In a country of individualists and lone wolves, where neighbours can be many miles away, *sisu* is a virtue of the first order. This is the ability to achieve one's aims with a pertinacity bordering on the stubborn. *Sisu* is definitely one of the reasons that Suomi is an ambitious industrial nation and counts as one of the world's most innovative and competitive countries. Children are equipped with the skills needed for a successful professional life on the international stage while at school. Just how successfully Finland does this, has been confirmed time and again in studies on educational standards. Even in their first year at school, for example, children have computer lessons and learn a foreign language. That's just as well really, as Finnish counts as an 'exotic' language. It is one of a small family of Finno-Ugric languages that are in danger of dying out. Anyone who seriously wants to get to know the Finnish culture in some depth, should at least try to learn a few words of this seemingly strange language – but you should also remember that Finns are happy to help visitors any time in English.

A tolerant people which is always willing to make compromises

For some 500 years the Finnish people were ruled by the Kingdom of Sweden. The upper classes spoke Swedish; Finnish was the language of farmers and foresters. Separated from the 'mainland' by the Baltic and with its 1200 km-long (750 mi) border with Russia, the region was often a bone of contention between the two major powers and fell to Russia in 1809. Its status as an autonomous 'Grand Principality' laid the cornerstone for the later nation of Finland. Helsinki became the seat of parliament, a national identity was kindled and the Finnish language was recognised as the second official language in 1863. Music and architecture developed a style of their own, too. In 1917, the Finns boldly declared independence during the October Revolution in Russia and were put to the hardest of tests on several occasions during the confusion of both world wars. Today, Finland is a parliamentary democracy and is one of the most stable societies in the world. The country is a committed member of the EU. Neutrality, the ability to compromise, reservation and tolerance characterise its political position.

Sometimes Finland is hastily passed off as being monotonous. To put it more succinctly: one has to like being on one's own to like the country. Those who need a lot of company will not feel at home here. At 16 people per km², the population density of Finland is very low; some areas of the country are extremely thinly populated and Lapland –

1939–1944
Finland has to concede large areas of its territory to Russia

1995
Finland becomes a member of the EU

2000
Tarja Halonen becomes the first woman to hold the office of President

2001
Introduction of smoking prohibition in public spaces

2008
Nobel Peace Prize is awarded to Martti Ahtisaari

2012
Helsinki is the World Design Capital –

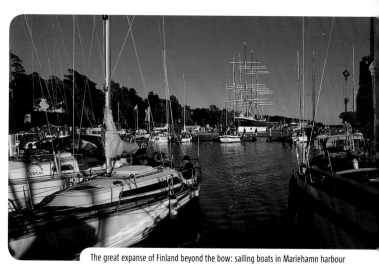

The great expanse of Finland beyond the bow: sailing boats in Mariehamn harbour

which after all makes up one third of the country – is virtually uninhabited. But this brings a lot of advantages with it. As a tourist, you can look forward to swimming and fishing as much as you like in clear lakes, and to breathing unpoluted air. Those who love Finland enjoy hiking for hours on end or going off on paddling tours through a natural environment which, although not always totally untouched, is still home to bears and eagles, wolves, otters and many other animals and plants. Millions of berries and mushrooms wait to be harvested every year. Restaurants cook with fresh, regional produce that frequently is organic in quality even if it comes without the official seal of approval. While environmental awareness is growing, Finland is,

The home of bears, wolves and eagles

however, not a 'green' fairy-tale country. Energy policies are based on nuclear power, marshlands are being drained on a large scale, forests chopped down and urban settlements often sprawl seemingly without any conscious planning into the surrounding countryside. The rapid rural exodus after World War II resulted in unimaginative blocks of flats being built in the middle of what were once idyllic towns.

By contrast, there are also very pretty corners to explore such as the wooden house districts in coastal towns. The culturally interested are more like to find what they are looking for in the wealthier south of the country with its country houses, art galleries and marinas than in the harsh, untamed north – although that also has its surprises in store, too. Suomi is fascinating and different, in its own unique way, wherever you go. Nowhere else is the light in the summer as bright and the lakes in the evening as peaceful as here. This is where you can take a deep breath and recharge your batteries. Welcome to Finland!

WHAT'S HOT

1 Underground

Helsinki's music scene They like partying and do it well! Those living in the capital have rediscovered dancehall music. Hidden in an inner courtyard, *Kuudes Linja* welcomes guests in party mood *(Hämeentie 13, www.kuudeslinja.com)*. In *Club YK*, DJs keep everyone on their toes *(Pohjoinen Rautatiekatu 21, www.clubyk.fi)*. *Kokomo Tikibar* is the ideal place to launch a night out on the town. DJs and dev-ilishly good drinks get the evening off to a good start *(Uudenmaankatu 16–20, www. kokomo.fi)*.

Fun fashion

2

More than just clothes Extra-long sleeves, patch-work patterns, bold prints and lacing: fashion running wild, like for example in *Shop Lux (Uudenmaankatu 26, Helsinki)* or the more grown-up creations at *Tiia Vanhatapio (Tiia Vanhatapio Couture Noir, Laivurinkatu 43, Helsinki)*. And whoever wants to check out the scene unnoticed can simply take a look at the style blog *www.hel-looks.com (photo)*, where fashion is really fun!

Chilly nights

3

Built on snow There are not only hotels built of snow in Finland but also complete wedding chapels, play-grounds and restaurants. In *Snow Village* in Ylläsjärvi it is not just the beds bathed in a red light that are made of ice, even the curtains and windows in the guesthouse and restaurant are made of frozen water. *(Ylläsjärventie 158, www.snowvillage.fi)*. In Lapland's Hotel Kakslauttanen, guests can choose between a roof of snow or glass: from the cosy bed with piles of pelts on it in an igloo, the second option provides a view of the northern lights *(Saariselkä, www.kakslauttanen.fi, photo)*.

The never-ending boom

Nordic creativity Finland – and especially its capital – has kept its reputation as a design nation. Helsinki is the World Design Capital 2012 *(www.worlddesigncapital.com)*, a title that the metropolis really has earned. And the *Design Museum* that traces the history of Finnish design and its creative protagonists *(Korkeavuorenkatu 23, Helsinki, www.designmuseum.fi)* just goes to prove this. Every summer during the *Helsinki Design Week* the creatively minded show the world the potential waiting to be tapped *(www.helsinki designweek.com, photo)*. Even more design events are planned for 2012. More information can be found under www.wdc2012helsinki.fi

Crazy contests

Inventive The Finns are considered slightly mad at times and have a reputation for strange competitions! And there are certainly enough examples to prove the point: the Wife-carrying and Mobile Phone Throwing World Championships, for example, are well known, but the Suomis are always thinking up new ones. One of the most famous and spectacular is the Air Guitar World Championship in August in Oulu *(www.airguitarworldchampion ships.com, photo)*. The idea for the Snowball Fight European Championship has been borrowed from Japan. It takes place in Yukigassen in Lapland where there is enough snow early in the year to ensure a good event *(Pöyliövaara Sports Arena, www.yukigassenfi. aazilla.com)*. The annual Mosquito Killing Contest however came about more out of necessity. In Pelkosenniemi in Lapland *(www.pelko senniemi.fi)*, each participant has five minutes to kill as many of the b(l)ighters as possible.

IN A NUTSHELL

ARCHITECTURE

The traditional house in Finland is of painted wood with white windows. Building with wood is something deeply rooted in the Finnish tradition and takes its lead from Nature in both shape and the materials used. Young, Finnish architects regularly steal the show with their innovate wooden buildings, such as the *Metlatalo* in Joensuu (Antti-Matti Siikala), the *Sibeliustalo* in Lahti (Hannu Tikka and Kimmo Lintula) and the *Kierikki Stone Age Centre* in Yli-Ii (Reijo Jallinoja). Alvar Aalto (1898–1976), with his characteristically organic and functional style, became internationally famous and exerted a strong influence on Finnish architecture for more than 30 years. For Finnish architects, building requires a comprehensive approach which is why many also design furniture and objects for everyday use.

BEARS

Ursus arctos, the brown bear, is Finland's national animal. Nobody knows exactly how many of this species live in Finland's forests – estimates are of around 1000 animals. Only in Russia are there more of these large predators and there are always visiting bears that wander across the border from Russia. Most bears in Finland live in Lapland or in the east of

Photo: Brown bear with cubs

Whether architecture or equal rights: the people in Finland have managed to bridge the gap between the traditional and the modern

the country. The chance of actually coming face to face with one is slight. Organised photo safaris are therefore popular – the guides know the bears' favourite spots. Bears are very shy when humans are around and avoid contact. When hiking through thinly populated areas it is recommended that you talk loudly or sing when walking through forests. Bears will then hear you coming and get out of the way.

However, should you ever meet a bear, do not make any hurried movements, run away or stare at it. Try to keep calm and slowly move backwards without ever turning your back on the animal.

DESIGN

Finnish designers draw on the natural Nordic environment for insipiration and generally do without anything superfluous.

Functional beauty in Helsinki Design Museum

school facilities and runs through the whole education system. Teaching aids are a matter of course, as are school lunches. If a child has learning difficulties, expert and psychological support is on hand so that everybody manages to make the grade together. Apart from classical academic subjects, equal importance is placed on sport and artistic ability. Both gifted pupils and those with learning and social deficits are given special supervision. And ever since the country has been at the top of the OECD Pisa study list, the Finnish education model is regarded as exemplary.

ELK

There are around 120,000 elk roaming around Finland. These bulky animals are a species of the deer family and, at a height of 2 m (6.5 ft) at the shoulder, are the largest kind of modern-day deer. These antler-bearing animals multiply extremely well in Finland's forests which means that a certain number of animals are allowed to be hunted every year to maintain a balanced ecological system. Elks are not particularly timid. The likelihood of meeting these imposing herbivores is high. For this reason you'll find red and yellow warning signs with an elk symbol on a lot of Finland's roads. Drivers should take this warning seriously as there are around 2000 accidents with elks every year. Most end fatally for the animal – some for humans.

Their seemingly reduced style, frequently including natural materials, stands for quality and a long service life. Whoever wants to take a closer look at Finnish design does not need to go to a museum. An invitiation to a Finnish home or a stroll around the shops is just as good. Designer articles in Finland are everyday objects that you can find and buy virtually everywhere. The best-known brands are *Arabia* and *Pentik* (ceramics), *Iittala* (glass), *Artek* (Aalto furniture and fittings), *Kalevala Koru* (jewellery with mythical symbols) and of course the textile company *Marimekko*, with its brightly coloured and boldly patterned printed fabrics.

EDUCATION

'Nobody should ever be left behind' – this is the motto of the Finnish state's education agenda. It starts with the family-friendly structure of day-care and nursery

EVERYMAN'S RIGHT

'Everyman's right' or the freedom to roam – as the name implies – is not just for Finns but for everyone. It is a common right that is shared by all Nordic countries and regulates what people can do in the countryside. According to this law, everyone can pick flowers, berries and mushrooms (provided they are not protected) and put up a tent on open ground for a brief period (as long as it is an 'appropriate' distance from the nearest habitation). A few of the other clauses include: if you want to fish with a stick and a hook, you don't need a fishing licence; hiking, cycling and skiing are allowed everywhere (unless that could risk damaging a crop in a field or a garden). However, the right to roam also has its limits. It is forbidden to camp or make a noise if this could effect others, to disturb nesting birds or other animals, or to collect wood for a campfire from private property. It is also generally not allowed to light an open fire in the middle of the countryside.

INDUSTRY

Finnish industry today is still firmly rooted in the tradition of the heroes in the national epic *Kalevala*. Even the mythical hero Held Väinämöinen (the protagonist in the epic poem) knew how to make boats unsinkable. Nowadays, it is icebreakers, luxury yachts and huge cruise liners that sail out of Finnish shipyards. One fairy-tale business history is that of Nokia. At the beginning of the 20th century, the company was making rubber boots; 100 years later mobile phones were coming off the conveyor belt and the firm had become market leader in the mobile communications branch – a position that the concern had to concede following the sweeping success of smartphones.

KALEVALA

The national epic *Kalevala* is the fist literary work written in Finnish. It is a collection of sagas and myths that had been passed down from one generation to the next as songs. Elias Lönnrot (1802–1884) spent many years travelling around Karelia, writing down thousands of lines of verse, sensing that runic singers would probably die out at the end of the 19th century. The first edition was published in 1835 and had a considerable influence on boosting the Finnish national identity. The epic is still very much in the public conscience and is an inspiration to both the average Finn as well as artists. It has been translated into numerous languages, and the easy-to-digest comic version by Mauri Kunnas can be found in every bookshop.

MINORITIES

The Sami people (*Sámi* or *Saami*) are the indigenous people of Lapland, living in an area that extends from Norway to the Kola Peninsula in Russia. In the course of time and as the various countries developed and changed, they were pushed further and further north. They now live from reindeer farming, fishing and tourism. Long considered second-class citizens, the 8000 Sami now enjoy legal protection in Finland. They are represented in parliament (*sámediggi*) and cultivate their language and culture. On special occasions they bring out their brightly-coloured traditional costumes and remind us of their natural religion with its belief in spirits and shamanism. However, the life of this indigenous people is still not without its conflicts to this day. Time and again there are problems with timber companies that destroy the reindeer's winter food supply – reindeer lichen – by clear felling whole swathes of land.

Another minority group in the country are the 'home-comers'. These are about 40,000 in number, most of whom are from East Karelia and now live in Finland. They speak Russian and the majority belongs to the Orthodox Church. A third group is the Romani people. About 10,000 live in Finland and their language is officially recognised as a minority tongue.

The 290,000 Swedish-speaking Finns live primarily on the west coast and in the island province of Åland. Strictly speaking, they are not a minority, as Swedish is the second official language in the country.

They are often attributed with the arrogance of the upper classes, as – traditionally – most wealthy families and the some 6000 aristocrats in Finland, speak Swedish. While the different peoples described here are integrated in society, it is becoming increasingly difficult for refugees.

MÖKKI

The summerhouse on the lake is the Finnish version of 'back to the roots'. There are more than half a million of these cabins. The *mökki* fits perfectly into the 'anti-stress' programme adopted by many who enjoy the simplicity of chopping up wood, picking berries, rowing, barbecuing, fishing and, of course, having a sauna and bathing in the lake. As not every family can afford to have such a holiday home these idyllic cabins are also available for rent all over the place.

MOOMINS

Even the very young know that Moominvalley, where the hippopotamus-like trolls live, is somewhere in Finland. They were dreamt up by the author Tove Jansson (1914–2001), who created the adventures of Moomintroll, his parents, the Snork Maiden and all the other friendly creatures between 1945 and 1970. Jansson's books have been translated into almost 40 languages and are still popular today. They have their own musem in Tampere, their own adventure park in Naantali and, every few years, the Finnish post office brings out Moomin stamps.

MUSIC

Jean Sibelius (1865–1957) is the great name in Finnish music. Like no other composer, he knew how to translate the moods of the Finnish countryside into a unique musical language as, for example, in his extremely melancholic 'Valse triste'. His music is closely associated with the emergence of the nation of Finland. The present music scene ranges from rock to jazz and from tango to humppa – the Finnish variant of the foxtrot. Humppa was long thought of as music for the older generation, but this changed in the mid 1990s when the band Eläkäläiset ('The Pensioners') brought humppa onto the international rock stage. Since then, this off-beat music, and with it the dance, is considered perfect for partying.

Another extremely popular type of music in Finland is heavy metal. Is it perhaps due to the pervading silence of the forests and the smooth-running state apparatus, that it can't be loud and noisey enough for many Finns? The number of rock groups – in relation to the population – is surprisingly high at any rate. Some bands, such as HIM, The Rasmus or Nightwish have also made it into international charts. One exception in this scene are the Leningrad Cowboys who call themselves 'the worst rock 'n' roll band in the world', but who – thanks to Aki Kaurismäki's film – have become famous nevertheless. And then there is Finnish tango music: the melancholic variation of Tango Argentino is to be heard up and down the country on every dance-floor and at every festival in the summer.

SAUNA

Simple and rooted in nature. These two attributes characterise the Finnish sauna – irrespective of whether it is in a little wooden cabin on the lakeside, on a campsite or in the sauna room of a rented block of flats. The Finns haven't come up with any rules or regulations like in many other countries. Nobody has to put up with towel-swinging 'sauna-officials' or the well-mannered silence, nor does anyone have to wait until the end of the steam ritual – when water is poured on the hot stones – before leaving the sauna. And nobody will blink twice if you wash your hair in

The Finns can best be found in their *mökkis* in the summer – this one is on Åland

the sauna or smoke ham over the wood-burning stove! Anything that anyone wants to do or is good for you is allowed. This includes the use of birch twigs *(vihta)* which you gently tap over your own body or someone else's – it doesn't only smell good, it also improves your blood circulation. Leering glances are totally taboo when sweating away in a sauna. And anyway, men and women are always segregated – there are no mixed-sex saunas in Finland. What there is, however, is a wide variety of different sauna types. There are saunas in buses and on trailers, electrical mini-variations for one-roomed flats and communal saunas in residential blocks with fixed sauna times. Even the early smoke sauna *(savusauna)* is experiecing a renaissance, following its virtually permanent disappearance as a result of fires frequently breaking out. And should it smell of tar after water has ben poured on the hot stones, then there is *löylyterva* (sauna tar) in the water which, along with vodka and hot cup therapy, is considered the third cure-all in traditional Finland.

WOMEN

Finnish women have the reputation of being strong-willed, self-assured and independent. Compared to other European countries, they also enjoy a good education and training. More than 90 percent have a job and can be found in all branches and on all hierarchical levels, except at the very top of industry. It is perfectly normal for mothers to be working full time. The state supports women's careers by providing sufficient kindergarten places with an all-round service. That there are no bars to Finnish women holding high official posts has been proven by Tarja Halonen in exemplary fashion. The lawyer held the office of President of the Republic of Finland from 2000 until 2012, working together with female ministers, female party leaders and female members of parliament as well. Women's involvement in politics has a tradition going back more than 100 years. In 1906, female Finns were the first women in Europe to be given the right to vote, both actively and passively.

FOOD & DRINK

Traditional Finnish cooking is nutritional and plain, intended to make sure that a hard-working population gets through the long, cold winter. Depending on the time of year, restaurants serve the typical Nordic range of home-grown food prepared to tried and tested recipes.

'Food fills you up', so many a Finn says – and a lot of dishes taste like that, too. The national cuisine really doesn't have the reputation of being star quality. But if you keep to traditional dishes and regional ingredients you will experience some praiseworthy culinary delights. On top of that, a lot of food is organic even if it does not come with a green stamp of approval –

especially in the far north. Fruit and vegetables grow a long way from any industrial centres or towns and are pollution free. And, obviously, the meat of wild animals comes from those roaming free in their natural habitat.

Due to the climate, the selection of native fruit and vegetables is limited, one could even say paltry. But the Finns are proud of what Nature has in store for them and of what they make with it. A snide remark by Italy's former prime minister, Silvio Berlusconi, about the Finnish cuisine a few years ago, triggered off a real cooking boom. Traditional ingredients like beetroot, swedes and white cabbage are now being

Photo: Crayfish – a Scandinavian speciality

Nature throws open her larder door: Finnish cooking brings the produce of the forests and the lakes to the table

ingeniously transformed into gourmet experiences. However, hotpots, soups, casseroles, roasts and pies still dominate everyday cooking.

International cuisine is only gradually making headway. The standard repertoire in the restaurant scene comprises Finnish, Scandinavian and Russian restaurants, but these are now being joined by pizzerias, Asian restaurants and the fast-food chain

Hesburger – a Finnish product. Vegetarian restaurants are still rare.

If you like fish, you'll enjoy going out for a meal. In a country with 200,000 lakes there are lots of excellent edible fish and a lot more off the coast as well.

A particular speciality can be sampled in January in the Kainuu region: eelpout soup. The animals' roe is served as caviar on blinis with sour cream. Ice fishing for

▶ **Blinis** – buckwheat pancakes filled with sour cream or mushrooms, among other ingredients

▶ **Graavi lohi** – gravad lax (marinaded salmon) with dill, to be found in every buffet and supermarket (photo, left)

▶ **Jokiravut** – the crayfish season runs from 21 July until well into September. The crustaceans are served with white wine and toast

▶ **Kalakukko** – rye pastry filled with filet of fish (perch, whitefish, herring), bacon and onions, available in Kuopio and in both outdoor and indoor markets

▶ **Karjalanpaisti** – Karelian pot roast with beef, lamb and pork as well as vegetables

▶ **Karjalanpiirakka** – slightly salted rice rolled inside a thin rye crust

▶ **Kesäkeitto** – milk-based summer soup with fresh vegetables and herbs

▶ **Liekki lohi** – grilled salmon. The whole fish is slit open, de-boned, nailed onto a piece of wood and grilled at the side of the fire

▶ **Lohikeitto** – light salmon soup, prepared with milk, potatoes, and dill

▶ **Mämmi** – Easter dessert made with malt, rye flour and orange peel

▶ **Mäti** – roe from the eelpout or whitefish, served with onions, sour cream and potatoes in their skin

▶ **Poronkäristy** – reindeer stew on mashed potato with cranberries

▶ **Runebergin torttu** – an individual cake, a favourite of the national poet Johan Ludvig Runeberg (photo, right), filled with almonds and topped with raspberry jam

▶ **Särä** – a lamb dish cooked in a long birchwood trough and traditionally served in Lemi near Lappeenranta

▶ **Voileipäkakku** – a filling sandwich cake made with bread, fish, mayonnaise and curd, a favourite on public holidays

pike, perch and bream starts as early as in March. Small whitefish that are commonly found in the lake district, are grilled whole – a typically Nordic speciality. On the coast you can savour wild salmon from the major rivers whereas salmon from a fish farm or rainbow trout is used by traditional Finns rather than whitefish for raw, salted filets. The beginning of the crayfish season on 21 July is a culinary highlight which, due to the diminishing number of crustaceans, is becoming an increasingly expensive treat. The summer is short and it is only after midsummer that the market stands start to fill up. Delicious strawberries, bilberries and raspberries – Finland is rich in such fruit – are longingly awaited. The yellow cloudberry, *lakka*, from the moors of Lapland, is a rare speciality. It is served as a dessert with junket and distilled to make a liqueur. If you want to know what a cloudbery looks like, keep your eyes open for a two-euro coin on which Lapland's emblem is shown.

Autumn is the best time to enjoy game. Traditional Finnish restaurants serve elk, reindeer and wild duck; Russian restaurants also have bear on the menu. Game can also be taken home in the form of salami or ham. This can be bought in the markets in Helsinki, for example.

What you will find to buy in abundance in Finland are sweet things. Chocolate (preferably from *Fazer*) keeps the northerners happy during the long winter months. The same goes for ice cream. No, this is not a misprint – Finns love their ice cream despite arctic temperatures. Berry cake and *pulla*, a dessert bread with crushed cardamom seeds, are also very popular. One dessert that you can expect to find in the most remote corner of any national park is *munkki*. This is a yeast-based bread sprinkled with sugar that is not dissimilar to a doughnut.

Kahvi ja munkki: you will see this sign outside every café and also many a restaurant, inviting you in for a snack. *Kahvi* means coffee – the Finnish national drink that is consumed in huge quantities. Finland heads the EU statistics for coffee consumption and, at almost 12 kilos per capita, is far ahead of anywhere else. By comparison, the Americans drink on average 4.2 kilos and the British a mere 2.8 kilos.

Lots of alcohol is also drunk but is still very expensive, especially in restaurants. An 'A' licence denote that all alcohol drinks can be served; a 'B' licence covers wine and

Every sunny day is enjoyed to the full: here on Aleksanterinkatu in Helsinki

beer; a 'C' licence just low-alcohol beer. High-proof beverages and wines are only available in branches of the Alko concern. If you want to sample Finnish gastronomy you may well find that you are locked out. Opening times and closing days are very varied throughout the country. There are some restaurants that are only open for lunch; others that open at 6pm, and many that are only open in summer. Generally speaking, the main meal of the day is a hot dinner in the evening that actually starts very early. If you go to a restaurant at around 5pm you will be bang on time. In major cities, restaurant kitchens, however, often stay open until midnight – but don't count on this in the country. And for those who would like to sample the traditional cooking and the local culture in a more personal way, click on *www.cosy finland.com* and book a meal in the private house of a Finnish host.

marimekko

SHOPPING

Finland is a mixture of village shop and American dream with US-style shopping 'malls' everywhere. Finland's largest ● 'Village Shop' *(tuuri kyläkauppa)*, which has up to 6 million visitors a year, is a mixture of the two *(near Ähtäri | www. tuuri.fi)*.

BOOKS & CDS

Music CDs and picture books as well as comics make good souvenirs. The *Akateeminen Kirjakauppa* (Academic Bookshop) in Helsinki *(Pohjoisesplanadi 39)* has a good selection of books in English.

DELICATESSEN & COSMETICS

Elk salami, reindeer ham, smoked salmon and marinaded fish, wines and liqueurs (all wineries: *www.viinitilat.net*) make perfect presents, as do jams made with local berries, chocolate and liquorice. Organic soaps with essential oils from *Aamumaa*, *Vihreakosmetiikka* or *Solavoima* are that little bit different. Sauna fans can stock up on everything from towels, tar shampoo or pine essence to felt hair protectors.

GLASS & CERAMICS

Major names such as the ceramics manufacturer *Pentik* and the glass company *Iittala* with their clear lines, are part of the very essence of Finnish design. Their products can be found in every departmental store and often in second-hand shops, too. The Pentik ceramics shop in Posio in Lapland is well worth a visit. You can pick up a bargain in the INSIDER TIP factory shop and then marvel at the coffee cups from around the world in the museum afterwards *(Oct–mid June Mon–Fri 10am–5pm, Sat/Sun 10am–4pm | Maaninkavaarantie 3 | www.pentik.com)*. Extravagant ideas can be bought in *Tonfisk* in Turku *(www. tonfisk-design.fi)*.

LAPLAND SOUVENIRS

Genuine products made by the Sami bear the *sami-duodji* stamp. Reindeer skins, boots, leather belts and bags are typical of Lapland, as is jewellery made from reindeer antlers and silverwork *(www. usvalintu.com, www.mta-sarviseppa.com)*. Young Sami are now producing more dar-

Nordic by nature: Elk salami, troll hats or soapstone are typical Finnish souvenirs

ing modern designs and fashion *(www. arcticpearls.fi, www.nativa.fi).*

METAL & JEWELLERY

Fiskars are razor sharp, handmade knives with wooden handles are sold by many master craftsmen (e.g. *www.kauhavanpuuk kopaja.fi, www.mvforge.fi*). Ultra-modern metal design by *Eero Hyrkäs* can be found in the Helsinki Design Forum or in the Vaprikki Museum Centre in Tampere.

TEXTILES

Marimekko does not just make fashions but peps up things such as oven gloves or flip-flops with a mixture of large floral motifs and bright colours. The Marimekko flagship store is located in Helsinki's design district *(Pohjoisesplanadi 31 | Kämp Gallerie)*. Things made of felt such as gloves,

troll hats and blankets are both attractive and warm. *Filtti* in Petäjävesi *(www.filtti.fi)* stocks works of art and accessories made of felt. Handmade lace comes from Rauma and young desingers now cheekily combine all sorts of different materials in their products *(www.class2004.com)*. Handwoven rugs, linen towels, pullovers and furs from home-reared animals, all have a long tradition in Finland.

WOOD

Polished bowls and birchwood mugs, servers or animals are typically Finnish. Birch bast is used to weave baskets and sauna lights are produced with cut-out motifs. Virtually every department store stocks a range of *Aarikka* wooden jewellery and decorative items. Furniture made by moulding wood can be found at Artek *(www.artek.fi)*.

THE PERFECT ROUTE

FOR CULTURE-VULTURES: START IN HELSINKI

Welcome to ① *Helsinki* → p. 32: The capital on the sea with its designer shops, interesting architecture (photo, left) and cultural avant-garde cannot fail to please. Take your time before heading for the metal production centre at ② *Fiskars Village* → p. 48, a living museum village with more than 100 active artists and designers. Carry on via Perniö, Kimito and Sauvo to ③ *Turku* → p. 60, the oldest town in the country with its castle, cathedral and floating restaurants along the river bank. Here, at the latest, you should have your bathing things at hand.

WATER AND LACE

The blue of the water and the green of the islands will be accompanying you for some time: the ④ *skerry circuit* → p. 94 should not be missed before you head for Uusikaupunki on your way to the old wooden town of ⑤ *Rauma* → p. 63. This World Heritage Site is also the home of lacemaking. The handmade lace is so delicate and light that you'll certainly have room for a piece in your suitcase.

ALL ABOARD FOR A CRUISE

150 km (93 mi) inland, you'll reach the first lakes and Finland's 'green heart': ⑥ *Tampere* → p. 75. Soak up the unique atmosphere of the restored factory buildings, the winding alleyways in the former workers' district and the stretches of water in the suurounding area. If you have a bit of time, take a mini cruise from Tampere on one of the boats operated by Finnish Silverline (Suomen Hopealinja Oy).

THE SUN ROUTE

Return to the sunny coast via Virrat and Jalasjärvi and on to Vaasa. You are now on the Sun Route than runs betwen Vaasa and Oulu and from Route 727 onwards offers beautiful views running up the coast. In ⑦ *Oulu* → p. 58 it is worth taking a break. Try the fish on the lively market square or take a ferry across to the natural paradise of Hailuoto.

VISITING SANTA CLAUS

The journey takes you further north. From ⑧ *Aavasaksa* → p. 93, a hill above the Tornio valley, you have a wonderful view across uninhabited Lapland. Carry on to Kolari and Muonio until you reach

Experience the diversity of Finland with detours to visit Santa Claus and to see the last remaining primeval forests in Europe

9 *Pallas-Yllästunturi National Park* → p. 93, where you can experience the peace and quiet of Lapland's fells before going on to **10** *Rovaniemi* → p. 91 by way of Levi and Kittilä. Drop in on Santa Claus and visit the prize-winning Arktikum museum that tells the story of the people and nature of the north.

THE BEAR TOUR

After a serving of reindeer stew you'll be perfectly prepared to head straight for the wilderness of Lapland. You can take a hike along the 'Bear's Ring' in one of the largest primeval forests in Europe in **11** *Oulanka National Park* → p. 86. From now on, your journey is through sheer endless forests until you reach **12** *Kuhmo* → p. 82. If you time your visit well, you will arrive for the famous chamber music festival.

COUNTRYSIDE AND MUSIC

From Kuhmo, the route takes you via Nurmes to the spectacular views to be had in **13** *Koli National Park* → p. 84. In the next few hours the countryside you will pass starts to change. The forest opens up into a landscape of lakes (photo, right) and will take you to **14** *Savonlinna* → p. 72, where the opera festival is held. The clever ones will have already booked a *mökki* in the Saimaa lake district and can

2850 km (1771 mi). Driving time only: 41 hours. Recommended time for this trip: 2 weeks. The detailed route is shown inside the back cover, in the road atlas and on the pull-out map

enjoy a few peaceful days or weeks. A trip to the medieval town of **15** *Porvoo* → p. 46 with its art galleries, boutiques and idyllic cafés provides a change of scenery. A further 50 km (31 mi) further on, and you're back in Helsinki again.

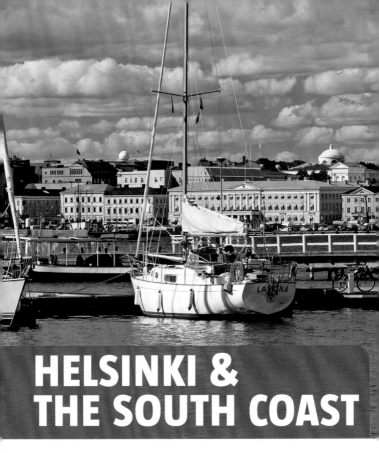

HELSINKI &
THE SOUTH COAST

The south coast mirrors the history and national identity of Finland. The capital city, Helsinki – a Finnish version of St Petersburg in miniature – lies in the middle of this stretch of coast, dividing it into almost equal halves to the west and east. The influence of the neighbouring countries that enriched cultural life in the south of Finland can still be felt today. Churches and ruined fortresses, country houses, ironworkers' settlements and harbours line the 'Royal Way', the *Kuninkaantie*, that follows the old mail coach route from Stockholm to St Petersburg. The harbours are gateways to the world. In summer, they are alive with yachts, fishing boats and barges; in winter the Finnish fleet of icebreakers makes sure that the waterways stay open to traffic. Helsinki, together with the towns of Espoo and Vantaa, forms an urban area with a population of 1.3 million.

HELSINKI

MAP INSIDE THE BACK COVER
(126 C5) (*Ⓜ E14*) The capital of Finland (population 590,000) is a small, lively metropolis without any skyscrapers. Despite all the hustle and bustle of a large city, it exudes a calm and friendly self composure, so typical of Finland.

Photo: Helsinki marina

'The Baltic's beautiful daughter': for visitors, Helsinki is the gateway to Finland, for Finns it is the gateway to the world

The core of the city, an architectural gem in a variety of historical styles, was built on granite peninsulas right on the sea. When arriving by ferry, the white cathedral and the golden dome of Uspenski Cathedral can be clearly seen as you sail past Suomenlinna Fortress. On dry land, the colourful Market Square on South Harbour is alive with fishmongers and vegetable stall holders, souvenir shops

CITY WHERE TO START?
Kauppatori: The Market Square **(U D4)** *(⌂ d4)* is close to the city centre. Ships drop anchor in South Harbour beyond Kauppatori and the station is only a short distance away on the tramline 3T. There are many multi-storey car parks.

The archaic 'Rock Church' has a truly unique atmosphere

and stands selling Finnish specialities. The elegant street, Esplanadi, leads from here to the centre and is both the place to meet and to promenade back and forth. Ice cream stands sell huge scoops, luxury shops promote the latest trends and cafés serve espresso and berry cake.

As soon as the sun appears, the people of Helsinki are out on the streets. Whether street musicians, business women, tourists, dock workers, students or mothers with their children, everyone enjoys this carefree atmosphere with its slightly Mediterranean feel.

The magnificent Classicist façades from the 19th century, the bombastic National Romanticism and the more than 600 Art Nouveau houses in the districts of Eira, Katajanokka and Kruununhaka give the city its special flair. The functionalist buildings are from the 1930s and the modern glass and steel constructions are more recent. The city's appearance is completed by the wooden house districts (Vallilla and Käpylä), the workers' district (Kallio) and the docks.

The city is a stage for avant-garde Finnish artists, for designers and business people. Major projects are boldly designed and executed without touching the charming centre. The 2012 World Design Capital also has a lot to offer culturally. Apart from the many designer shops and art galleries, there is everything from first-class classical music to rock, and from modern dance to stand-up comedy. The nightlife is vibrant, the 'in' scene not too extensive and therefore pleasantly intimate.

All major sights can easily be reached on foot or with the tram 3T – part of the city's very popular and well-maintained cultural heritage. The transition from the town to the country is also very easy. Helsinki, 'the Baltic's beautiful daughter', is surrounded by sandy beaches and islands. Fans of the great outdoors can look forward to cycling and sailing in the area.

SIGHTSEEING

ATENEUM (U C4) (*ⓜ c4*)

Finland's oldest art museum is stylishly housed in a magnificent neo-Renaissance building from 1887 and holds the largest collection of Finnish classical art from the 18th century to the 1960s. *Tue/Fri 10am–6pm, Wed/Thu 10am–8pm, Sat/Sun 11am–5pm | 9 euros | Kaivo-katu 2 | on the square outside the station | www.ateneum.fi*

KAIVOPUISTO (FOUNTAIN PARK) ☼ (U D–E6) (*ⓜ d–e6*)

The large park adjoining the ambassadors' district in the south-east of the city was laid out in 1830 as a spa park. From the rocks near the Ursa observatory you have a lovely view of the islands and marina. The club restaurant *Kaivohuone*, with its swim-

ming pool, large terraces, bars and VIPs, is a top address in summer for night-owls.

ESPLANADI ★ (U C–D4) (*ⓜ c–d4*)

All the well-known shops such as Marimekko, Artek, etc. as well as hotels can be found on this green boulevard behind the magnificent façades of the buildings along the twin main shopping streets *Pohjoi* and *Etelä-Esplanadi*. The bronze statue *Havis Amanda,* created in 1908 by Ville Valgren, is at the eastern end. The naked maiden, a symbol of the city, was highly controversial when first unveiled. Every year on 1 May, it is given a student cap to wear.

TEMPPELIAUKION KIRKKO (ROCK CHURCH) ● (U B3) (*ⓜ b3*)

The sunken church, designed by the two architects and brothers Timo and Tuomo Suomalainen and opened in 1969, was blasted out of the granite bedrock. The natural rock walls support a huge dome

★ **Esplanadi**
Helsinki's grand boulevard with lots of cafés → p. 35

★ **Seurasaari**
Finland's largest midsummer festival is held every year on this island, 5 km (3 mi) from the centre. It's other major attraction is the wonderful open-air museum → p. 36

★ **Senaatintori (Senate Square)**
Grand Neoclassicist architecture on Senate Square with Helsinki Cathedral → p. 37

★ **Suomenlinna**
The Swedish fortress on an island is a World Heritge Site → p. 38

★ **Design District**
Helsinki's creative heart: classic 25 roads where Finnish designers as well as newcomers can be found → p. 41

★ **Kauppatori (Market Square)**
The best place to start exploring Helsinki → p. 41

★ **Porvoo**
Little, medieval, wooden town from the 14th century located on a river → p. 46

★ **Fiskars Ironworks & Village**
Art, design and crafts in a historic village near Pohja → p. 48

MARCO POLO HIGHLIGHTS

of copper wire and glass. The best way to experience this space is at a concert or church service. *Mon/Wed 10am–5pm, Thu/Fri 10am–8pm, Tue 10am–12.45pm and 2.15pm–5pm, Sat 10am–6pm, Sun 11.45am–1.45pm and 3.30pm–6pm | free admission | Lutherinkatu 3, Töölö*

FINLANDIATALO (FINLANDIA HALL)
(U B3) (*b3*)

The congress and concert house by Alvar Aalto was completed in 1971 and is considered to be the epitome of the Finnish architect's functional architectural style. The silhouette of Carrara marble on the southern shore of Töölö Bay has become one of the city's landmarks. *Only guided tours available, every Wed (2pm) | 11 euros | Mannerheimintie 13E*

PÄÄRAUTATIEASEMA (MAIN RAILWAY STATION) (U C3) (*c3*)

This imposing and stylistically unusual building by Eliel Saarinen has formed the heart of the public transport system for both local and long-distance trains since 1919. The four large sculptures of male figures on the main façade, each carrying a globe-shaped light in their hands, have been famously and effectively used for advertising purposes. *Kaivokatu*

ISLANDS (0)

The people of Helsinki are lucky indeed. Whenever they want to get out of the city, an island is never far away. You won't have it to yourself, but there are beaches for swimming and sunbathing, lovely paths and well-looked after summer restaurants. The most popular island – some 5 km (3 mi) north-west of the centre, is ★ *Seurasaari*. A wooden bridge links it with the mainland. The principal attraction is the open-air museum *(June–Aug daily 11am–5pm | 6 euros | bus 24 from the centre)*. Historical buildings from all over

Finland, including old farmhouses and a pretty little church, can be found here. Concerts and festivals are frequently held on Seurasaari. On the longest day of the year, people come here to celebrate midsummer around a campfire with dancing and music: ● the largest bonfire in Helsinki is lit here on the weekend after 21 June. Another equally popular island is *Särkkä*. The island restaurant helps promote that summer feeling: you can order picnic hampers there if you like. *(Jetty at Café Ursula | tel. 09 13 45 67 56 | Expensive)*. A little piece of paradise is *Tervasaari* island that can be reached on foot, with a restaurant, *Savu (Tervasaarenkannas 3 | tel. 09 74 25 55 74 | Moderate)*.

KIASMA (MUSEUM OF MODERN ART)
(U C3) (*c3*)

Kiasma is the Finnish form of the word 'chiasma', meaning 'hybrid'. The name picks up on the museum's futuristic architecture that stands out thanks to its rounded alu-

minium and glass construction. Contemporary art, mostly works by Finnish and Scandinavain artists are on display. *Tue 10am–5pm, Wed–Fri 10am–8.30pm, Sat/Sun 10am–6pm | 7 euros, free admission under 18 | Mannerheiminaukio 2*

KRUUNUNHAKA (U D–E3) (ᗰ d–e3)
Rauhankatu 1, regarded as the 'Pearl of Kruununhaka' and the most beautiful Art Nouveau building in the city, is located in the Art Nouveau district immediately behind the cathedral. And while you're in the vicinity: in *Kolme Kruunua (daily | tel. 09 135 41 72 | Liisankatu 5 | Budget–Moderate)*, the best meatballs in town have been served since 1952.

KANSALLISMUSEO (NATIONAL MUSEUM) (U B3) (ᗰ b3)
Frescos by the painter Akseli Gallen-Kallela with motifs taken from the national epic *Kalevala*, can be seen in the domed hall in the granite building from 1916, constructed in the National Romantic style. Finnish history from the Stone Age to the present day is displayed here. *Tue 11am–8pm, Wed–Sun 11am–6pm | 7 euros | Mannerheimintie 34*

SENAATINTORI (SENATE SQUARE) ★ (U D4) (ᗰ d4)
The square is one of the most beautiful examples of Neoclassical architecture anywhere. Tsar Alexander II ordered the government quarter of his new Finnish capital to be constructed to the designs of the German architect C. L. Engel between 1820 and 1850. An equestrian statue of the Tsar stands at the foot of an imposing flight of steps that leads up to the white *Tuomiokirkko*, the cathedral, of 1852 that dominates the surrounding area *(daily 9am–6pm, June–Aug until midnight)*. A wonderful view of the harbour and the square with the parliament building, the university and university library can be had from the ⤳ cathedral terrace.

Polished chrome: road cruisers on Senate Square in Helsinki

World Heritage Site: the fortress island Suomenlinna is still inhabited today

SIBELIUS MEMORIAL (U A2) *(ᗰ a2)*

The sculpture made of 600 steel pipes as a celebration of Jean Sibelius' music was not well received when first unveiled in 1967 – and the sculptor, Eila Hiltunen, had to supply a bust of the composer that was added later. Today, the 'steel pipe organ' in Sibelius Park is the most-photographed of the some 400 sculptures dotted around Helsinki. *At the northern end of Mechelininkatu*

KAUPUNGINMUSEO
(MUNICIPAL MUSEUM) (U D4) *(ᗰ d4)*

You can find out everything about Helsinki's history here. The nine branches of the museum include *Sederholm House (Aleksanterinkatu 16–18),* the oldest building constructed of stone in the city dating from 1757, and the *Burgher's House (Kristianinkatu 12),* the oldest wooden building in Helsinki (1818). *Main muse-um: Mon–Fri 9am–5pm, Sat/Sun 11am–5pm | free admission | Sofiankatu 4 | www.helsinkicitymuseum.fi*

SUOMENLINNA ⭐ (0)

A 20-minute ferry ride takes you to the island fortress of Suomenlinna, 'Finland's castle'. The complex was to be a stronghold against Russia – but to no avail. In 1809 Finland fell to Russia and the fortress became a garrison settlement for the Russians. It is now a World Heritage Site and an official city district with several houses, as well as being a recreational area and popular destination for outings. There are restaurants and cafés, a submarine, three galleries, twisting paths and picnic areas. A visitors' centre and five museums provide information about its history *(May–Sept daily 10am–6pm, Oct–April 10.30am–4.30pm | 5 euros).* Cross with the HKL ferry *(tickets for local transport network* valid) from *Kauppatori* | no. of crossings: 3 times an hour | duration approx. 20 min.

USPENSKI KATEDRAALI (USPENSKI CATHEDRAL) (U E4) (*Ø e4*)

Surrounded by Art Nouveau buildings and the docks in the *Katajanokka* district is the largest Orthodox church in western Europe (1868). Its golden dome is a reminder of the role Russia played in the country's history and its influence today. *Wed–Fri 9.30am–4pm, Tue 9.30am–6pm, Sat 9.30am–2pm, Sun noon–3pm, May–Sept also Mon 9.30am–4pm | Kanavakatu 1*

FOOD & DRINK

ATELJÉ FINNE (U B3) (*Ø b3*)

Delicious meat and fish dishes in the 'new Finnish style' are served in the former studio of the sculptor Jalmari Finne. Good selection of wines sold by the glass. Speciality: liquorice crème brûlée. *Closed Sun/Mon | Arkadiankatu 14 | tel. 09 49 31 10 | Moderate–Expensive*

CAFÉ EKBERG ● (U C5) (*Ø c5*)

This Swedish family-run business has been baking its own bread and cakes since 1852. The daily breakfast buffet is a much-visited highlight, the décor is nostalgic and cosy. *Daily | Bulevardi 9*

CAFÉ URSULA (U D4) (*Ø d4*)

Looking across the water seated in the shade under a sail: Ursula is a café on the shore with a long tradition on *Kaivopuisto*. Good lunch buffets, view across to Suomenlinna from the lovely terrace. *Daily | Ehrenströmintie 3 | www.ursula.fi*

CHEZ DOMINIQUE (U D4) (*Ø d4*)

This gourmet restaurant can boast two Michelin stars. The head chef, Hans Välimäki, conjures up artistically arranged culinary experiences in the French/

Scandinavian style. *Closed Sun/Mon | Rikhardinkatu 4 | tel. 09 6 12 73 93 | www.chezdominique.fi | Expensive*

ESPLANAD (U C4) (*Ø c4*)

If you like seeing and being seen, this is the right place. This popular terrace on the Esplanadi is a stage for the those going to the coffee house. Usually full, but even when not it is cosy. *Daily | Pohjoisesplanadi 37*

JUURI ☺ (U D5) (*Ø d5*)

Have you already tried *sapas*? This Finnish variant of tapas is made with regional ingredients – like many other dishes at Juuri's. Juuri is Finnish for 'root' – back to Finnish roots is the concept behind the restaurant business. The affiliated shop sells cheese, cold meats, vegetables and

LOW BUDGET

▶ A day-ticket for the local transport system is well worth it: 1 day costs 6.80 euros, 7 days 27.20 euros. The city tour on tram nos. 3T or 3B is the cheapest way to see things.

▶ The *Kaffecentralen* outlets serve good coffee for just 1 euro. And if you bring your own cup, you can even save another 50%. Branches: *Pursimiehenkatu 23, Korkeavuorenkatu 25, Museokatu 9*

▶ Eat and save: that's only possible with the coupon booklet *Eat Helsinki (30 euros)*. Using the coupons means that a second person can eat free of charge. The booklet is available from the *Academic Bookshop*, among other places (*Pohjoisesesplandi 39*)

handmade, regional products. *Daily | Korkeavuorenkatu 27 | tel. 09 63 57 32 | www.juuri.fi | Moderate*

KARLJOHAN (U C4) (*ᗰ c4*)
This restaurant is well-known for its light French/Finnish cuisine. One speciality is something that is found throughout Finland, *vorschmack*, an hors d'œuvre made of minced meat, herring and onions with crème fraîche. *Closed Sun | Yrjönkatu 21 | tel. 09 6 12 11 21 | www.ravintolakarljohan. fi | Moderate–Expensive*

INSIDER TIP KONSTAN MÖLJA (U B5) (*ᗰ b5*)
Finnish dishes made by a friendly couple with a love of cooking who know how to balance different tastes and present food perfectly. *Closed Sun | Hietalahdenkatu 14 | tel. 09 6 94 75 04 | Moderate*

MARTTA (U B4) (*ᗰ b4*)
The Association of Finnish Farmers' Wives serves up chanterelle soup, elk steak and zander in a rye crust, crisp salads and good children's meals. Bright, inviting and friendly. *Closed Sun | Lapinlahdenkatu 3 | tel. 050 5 11 80 88 | Moderate*

PERHO (U A4) (*ᗰ a4*)
Since 1932 this has been the restaurant attached to the first Finnish catering school. Menu changes daily, friendly service and home-brewed beer. *Daily | Mecheleninkatu 7 | tel. 09 58 07 86 49 | Budget–Moderate*

SASLIK (U D5) (*ᗰ d5*)
Russian nostalgia from the Tsarist era: blinis, borscht and bear steak. *Closed Sun | Neitsytpolku 12 | tel. 09 74 25 55 00 | Moderate (bear: Expensive)*

SAVOY 🔅 ☺ (U D4) (*ᗰ d4*)
This roof-top restaurant is well-known for its spectacular view over Helsinki and for

its furnishings by Alvar und Aino Aalto that have remained unaltered since 1937. The Savoy is considered one of the best restaurants in the world. Chef de cuisine Kai Kallio composes classical Finnish dishes with ingredients from organic farms or the restaurant's own roof garden. *Closed Sun | Eteläesplanadi 14 | tel. 09 61 28 53 00 | www.royalravintolat.com/savoy | Expensive*

INSIDER TIP ZUCCHINI (U D4) (*ᗰ d4*)
For vegetarians: small, cosy restaurant serving lunches only, soup of the day and one main course. *Closed Sat/Sun | Fabianinkatu 4 | tel. 09 6 22 29 07 | Budget*

SHOPPING

It's easy to go on a shopping spree around Helsinki. Small businesses sell handmade articles and even the big shops try to be individual. ● Stockmann (U C4) (*ᗰ c4*), the largest and oldest department store in the city, sells made-to-measure gentlemen's shoes, for example. The shop, founded in 1862, is an institution and has everything in stock that the stylish city customer could want (*Aleksanterinkatu 52*).

Thanks to the many arcades, shopping is even pleasurable in the Finnish winter or when it rains. The glass *Kamppi Center* (U B–C4) (*ᗰ b–c4*) complex that, combined with the Forum (*Mannerheimintie 20*), boasts 250 boutiques, eateries and shops, is both centrally located and ultra modern. The *Kämp Gallery (Pohjoisesplanadi 31)* (U D4) (*ᗰ d4*) is elegant and exclusive.

Ideas as to where to shop can be found in the free publications *Helsinki this Week, We are Helsinki* and *Nordic Oddity*. The favourite addresses of those from Helsinki include the music stores on *Viisikulma Square*, *Kenkäfriikki (Kluuvikatu 3)* (U D4) (*ᗰ d4*) for shoe freaks or the well-stocked second-hand bookshop *Hagelstam (Frede-*

rikinkatu 35) (U C5) (🗺 *c5*). Bookworms head straight for the *Academic Bookshop* (U C4) (🗺 *c4*), designed in the Alvar Aalto style (*Pohjoisesplanadi 39*).

DESIGN DISTRICT
⭐ (U B–D 4–5) (🗺 *b–d 4–5*)

A black dot in a white square is the symbol used by the consortium of 190 designers, artists and companies who are passionate about creative design. Small boutiques, jewellery studios, furniture designers and recycling art shops with this sticker in the window are particularly prevalent in *Uudenmaankatu* and in *Erottaja*. The *Designforum* (*Erottajankatu 7*) showcases young talented designers and unusual articles as well as serving coffee, too, in designer cups, of course. *www.designdistrict.fi*

MARKETS
⭐ *Kauppatori* (U D4) (🗺 *d4*) on South Harbour, with its mixture of fish and veg- etables, souvenirs and fast-food outlets, is the largest and most popular market in Helsinki. The pretty market halls in *Hakaniementori* (U D2) (🗺 *d2*) are the perfect place for sampling Finnish delicacies. Popular at lunchtime (INSIDER TIP the soups are excellent: *soppakeittiö*). *Töölöntori* (U A–B2) (🗺 *a–b2*), at the northern end of Runeberginkatu, is a small vegetable market where everything is absolutely fresh. 'Much loved' pieces of designer furniture at collectors' prices are a speciality in the market building at *Hietalahdentori* (U B5) (🗺 *b5*). A large flea market is held right outside at weekends in summer.

SPORTS & ACTIVITIES

SWIMMING
There are lots of different places to swim around Helsinki. The largest sandy beach is at Hietaranta (0) in Etu-Töölö. A popular

Fresh Finnish produce at Kauppatori market on South Harbour

Elegant: the Helsinki Day Spa

WATER SPORTS

Natura Viva Vuosaari (tel. 050 3 76 85 85 | www.seakayakfinland.com) and the *Helsinki Canoe Centre (Rajasaarenpenger 8 | tel. 09 4 36 25 00)* have kajaks to hire and organise canoe tours around the skerries. Unfurl the sails and cast off on the two-masters at the Helsinki `INSIDER TIP` Sailing Ships at Pohjoisranta, near Halkolaituri. After leaping into the sea you can have a sauna in the evening followed by a meal. Groups hire the complete ship; in July individuals can join in for 260 euros/day. *Helsingin Purjelaivakonttori, Pohjoisranta 8 | tel. 09 6 86 00 80 | www.purjelaiva.fi*

SPAS

The wood-fired `INSIDER TIP` Kotiharju Sauna (U D–E1) (*m d–e1*) in the workers' district, Kallio, offers a traditional Finnish spa packet with scrub, manicure and pedicure, massage or hot cup treatment (reservations necessary). *Tue–Fri 2pm–8pm, Sat 1pm–7pm | 10 euros | Harjutorinkatu | tel. 09 7 53 15 35 | www.kotiharjunsauna.fi.* The range of facilities in the modern and elegant *Helsinki Day Spa* (U C4) (*m c4*) includes Far-Eastern and Finnish massages, aromatherapy and osteopathy, and is the perfect place to let yourself be pampered. *Erottaja 4 | tel. 09 6 85 06 30 | www.dayspa.fi*

ENTERTAINMENT

CULTURE

Theatre, dance or ballet? The classical cultural venues in Helsinki boast an impressive and extensive repertoire. Whether it is the *Philharmonic Orchestra (www.hel.fi/filharmonia)*, the *Symphony Orchestra (www.yle.fi/rso)* or the *Sibelius Academy (www.siba.fi)* – they all maintain a traditional and classical modern repertoire of world-class standard. Ballet and modern dance are also performed at the *Opera*

place to go for a swim is on the island of *Pihlajasaari* (O) – journey time: 20 mins from Café Carusel. Once there, you will find a café and a place for barbecues as well as a nudist area. In the indoor swimming pool *Yrjönkadun Uimahalli* (U C4) (*m c4*), you can swim and take a sauna under Roman-style columns. *Opening times for men: Tue and Thu 6.30am–9pm as well as Sat 8am–9pm; women: Mon noon–9pm, Wed/Fri 6.30am–9pm and Sun noon–9pm | Yrjönkatu 21B | 12 euros | tel. 09 310 87401*

CYCLING

The *Helsinki cycle map (from the tourist information office)* suggests three excellent tours around the city and the surrounding area. Bikes can be hired at *Greenbike (Bulevardi 32 | www.greenbike.fi)* and *Ecobike (Savilankatu 1b, near the Olympic Stadium | www.ecobike.fi)*, among other places.

House (www.opera.fi). A total of ten theatres present classical drama and contemporary plays. Tip: on Saturdays the Finns have a good laugh at the cabaret and comedy shows put on in the Studio Pasila in the city theatre (www.ht.fi). A silver INSIDER TIP culture tram with an alternating programme of events runs Tue–Thu (3pm–6pm) along line 7A.

NIGHTLIFE

Young night-owls congregate in the district of Kallio (U C–D1) (ᗰ c–d1), intellectuals in Rytmi (Toinen Linja 2), clubbers in Kuudes Linja (Hämeentie 13). The Soul Kitchen helps prevent you getting hungry until 2am (Fleminginkatu 26–28). The under 25s amuse themselves in Töölö (0) in the Korjaamo tram depot (Töölönkatu 51b) or in Manala (Dagmarinkatu 2). Politicians are often spotted in the Storyville Jazzclub (Museokatu 8). Creative types and the media crowd head for the numerous 'in' places in Punavuori (U B–C 4–5) (ᗰ b–c 4–5). A stylishly relaxed atmosphere can be found in the city centre in the Apollo-Live Club (Mannerheimintie 16) (U C4) (ᗰ c4), in the panelled Redrum (Vuorikatu 2) (U D4) (ᗰ d4) with its good music, or in the On the Rocks bar (Mikonkatu 15) (U C4) (ᗰ c4). Painful renderings and new discoveries can be found in the karaoke bar Pataässä (Mariankatu 9) (U D4) (ᗰ d4) or in the seclusion of the massively popular ● INSIDER TIP karaoke taxi (www.karaoketaxi.fi).

TICKETS

The central Finnish ticket service is called Lippupalvelu (tel. 0600 10 8 00 (*) | www.lippupalvelu.fi). Less mainstream dance performances, concerts and festivals can be found in the Cable Factory (www.kaapelitehdas.fi) – the largest self-funding cultural centre in northern Europe.

WHERE TO STAY

If you have time to stay, the accommodation service in the main railway station can

BOOKS & FILMS

▶ **The Year of the Hare** – in books such as this one, Arto Paasilinna, a master of weird humour, depicts the Finnish man caught between heaven, nature and social hell

▶ **Saga. 35 Years of Photographs** – figures and landscapes merge into a work of art in Arno Rafael Minkkinen's black-and-white photographs, that could not be more Finnish

▶ **The Man Without a Past** – a man loses his memory and almost his life, but struggles to piece it together in his typically stoical and taciturn way. For this work, Aki Kaurismäki was awarded the Grand Prix at the 2002 Cannes Film Festival

▶ **The Cuckoo** – a masterpiece by the Russian director Alexander Rogoschkin (2002). A Russian, a Finn and a Sami woman – with no common language to speak – meet by chance in Finnish Lapland at the end of World War II.

▶ **Christmas Story** – the touching film (2007) by Juha Wuolojoki, with beautiful images of Lapland, explaining how Santa Claus came to be Father Christmas

help *(tel. 09 22 88 14 00)*. There is a wide range of places to choose from in summer. It is usually cheaper booking online.

CAMPING RASTILA (0)

Campsite in Vuosaari with cabins and fully-equipped holiday homes, summer hostel, sauna with beach (ice swimming in winter), bikes and kajaks for rent. *Open all the year round | tel. 09 31 07 85 17 | www.rastilacamping.fi | Budget*

CITYKOTI APARTMENT HOTEL (U B4) (𝄐 b4)

A stay of just two or more days makes these fully-equipped, self-catering apartments a reasonably priced alternative. *Malminkatu 38 | tel. 050 5 55 00 58 | www.citykoti. com | Budget–Moderate*

EUROHOSTEL (U F4) (𝄐 f4)

Reasonable, clean and friendly, youth-hostel style accommodation with a morning sauna in Katajanokka. *255 beds | Linnankatu 9 | tel. 09 6 22 04 70 | www. eurohostel.fi | Budget*

HOSTEL ACADEMICA (0)

Modern youth hostel near beach; all rooms with shower, WC and kitchenette, morning sauna with pool. *159 beds | Hietaniemenkatu 14 | tel. 09 13 11 43 34 | www. hostelacademica.fi | Budget–Moderate*

HOTEL FABIAN (U D5) (𝄐 d5)

Boutique hotel in the middle of the city. Contemporary interior design, big breakfasts and very friendly service. *20 rooms | Fabianinkatu 7 | tel. 09 61 28 20 00 | www. hotelfabian.fi | Moderate*

HOTEL GLO (U D4) (𝄐 d4)

Luxury hotel with day spa and large, modern and stylishly furnished rooms. *144 rooms | Kluuvikatu 4 | tel. 09 58 40 95 40 | www.hotelglo.fi | Expensive*

HOTEL HELKA (U B4) (𝄐 b4)

Stylishly furnished with Finnish designer classics. Good value for money. *150 rooms | Pohjoinen Rautatiekatu 23 | tel. 09 61 35 80 | www.helka.fi | Moderate*

KÄMP (U D4) (𝄐 d4)

A luxury hotel from 1887. Where Jean Sibelius composed and where today's stars like Madonna or Lady Gaga stay. Every inch is infused with Finnish history, fame and elegance. The service is to match. *179 rooms | Pohjoisesplanadi 29 | tel. 09 57 61 11 | www.hotelkamp.fi | Expensive*

SOKOS HOTEL TORNI (U C4) (𝄐 c4)

This traditional hotel has been recently renovated and its comfortable rooms are now available in three styles: Art déco, Jugendstil or simply functional. The legendary ☀ INSIDER TIP ▶ Ateljee Bar on the 14th floor has excellent cocktails and – sorry, guys – the 'Ladies' has the best view of the city. *152 rooms | Yrjönkatu 26 | tel. 020 123 46 04 | www.sokoshotels.fi/ hotellit/helsinkitorni | Expensive*

INFORMATION

One of the tourist information office's (U D5) (𝄐 d5) free brochures is a 😊 map *Walk the green Helsinki* which marks seven different routes for exploring Helsinki on foot. *Pohjoisesplanadi 19 | 09 31 01 33 00 | www.visithelsinki.fi und www.hel.fi*

WHERE TO GO

ESPOO (126 B5) (𝄐 E14)

Finland's second largest town (pop. 250,000) is 16 km (10 mi) to the west and stretches out between woods and fields, lakes and the sea. The *university* bears the stamp of Alvar Aalto. The *WeeGee Exhibition Centre (Tue–Sun | 10 euros | Ahertajantie 5 | www.weegee.fi)* with its

The red Ferrari comes as no surprise: many famous faces stay at Kämp

five museums, including the *Emma,* the Museum of Modern Art, is very popular. The Nuuksio National Park is also part of Espoo. A 4 km-long (2½ mi) *Haukankierros* (Hawks' tour) *circular route* leads to a ⚡ rocky outcrop and viewpoint.

HVITTRÄSK (126 A5) (*ɖ D13*)

30 km (18½ mi) away is the beautiful Art Nouveau ensemble (from 1902) where the Finnish architects Eliel Saarinen, Herman Gesellius and Armas Lindgrén lived and worked, surrounded by beautiful country-side on Lake Hvitträsk. Exhibitions, a restaurant and a café. *May–Sept daily 11am–6pm, otherwise Tue–Sun 11am–5pm | 5 euros*

LAHTI (126 C4) (*ɖ E13*)

The town (pop. 100,000, 106 km (65 mi) from Helsinki) is an international winter sports' centre where many skiing compe-titions are held. In summer, the ⚡ large ski jump is turned into a viewpoint *(June–Aug Mon–Fri 10am–5pm, Sat/Sun 11am–5pm | 8 euros, Ski Museum included in price).* Lahti is also a good place to take a boat trip to Jyväskylä or into Päijänne National Park. Before you set off, take a look at the famous concert hall, ● the *Sibelius Hall,* on the harbour – an im-posing wooden building with a glass mantle *(Mon–Fri 8–5pm | free admission | Ankkurikatu 7 | www.sibeliustalo.fi).*

Another piece of Finland – less famous but that much stranger – can be found in *Kariniemi Park.* Twelve, large INSIDER TIP human-shaped sculptures are slowly be-ing taken over by nature. They were cre-ated and put here by the artist Olavi Lanu. For many years they have been left to the whims of the seasons and are sometimes hidden by leaves or draped in icicles. Tourist information office: *Lahti Travel Ltd. | Rautatienkatu 22 | tel. 0207 28 17 50 | www.lahtitravel.fi*

PORVOO

(126 C5) (*E13*) ⭐ **Finland's second oldest town (pop. 48,000) is 50 km (31 mi) east of Helsinki. Wooden houses huddle picturesquely onto the valley slopes above the river, red warehouses flank the bank and museums, cafés, art galleries and little shops lie hidden in the labyrinth of courtyards.**

Porvoo has inspired many important Finnish artists over the centuries. To this day, there is still an artists' colony in the town. Its proximity to Helsinki makes Porvoo the most popular place for those living in the capital to go for a day trip.

SIGHTSEEING

OLD TOWN AND CATHEDRAL

The well-kept wooden town from the 14th century looks like a time capsule with its cobbled streets and enchanting gardens. The cathedral from 1418 sits majestically on the hilltop. Its whitewashed stone walls contrast with the black wooden shingle roof and its brick ornamentation *(May–Sept Mon–Fri 10am–6pm, Sat 10am–2pm, Sun 2pm–5pm, Oct–April Tue–Sat 10am–2pm, Sun 2pm–4pm | Kirkkotori 1)*

RUNEBERG HOUSE MUSEUM

The museum provides an insight into the everyday family life of Finland's national poet Johan Ludvig Runeberg (1804–1877). On the revered poet's birthday, on 5 February, the cafés in Porvoo and the rest of the country serve *Runeberg cakes* – a sweet cake with almonds and raspberry jam. As the story goes, the poet is reputed to have had a cake and a glass of punch every day for breakfast. *May–Aug Tue–Sun 10am–4pm, Sept–April Wed–Sun 10am–4pm | free admission | Aleksanterinkatu 3*

FOOD & DRINK

CAFÉ CABRIOLE

Delicious lunch buffets and an excellent selection of cakes. *Daily | Piispankatu 30 | tel. 019 5 23 28 00 | Budget*

Picturesque Porvoo: the wooden houses on the river are a testimony to days gone by

FREDRIKAN LÄHDE ☺
Vegetarian lunches, organic bread and, if required, a message *(40–60 euros/hour)*. *Runeberginkatu 18 | Mon–Fri 11am–3pm, Sat noon–3pm | tel. 040 8 28 88 89 | Budget*

WANHA LAAMANNI
For years, this restaurant on the hill near the cathedral has been a firm fixture on the list of the top 50 restaurants in Finland. Gourmet meat and fish dishes served in a wooden barn dating from 1790. *Daily | Vuorikatu 17 | tel. 020 7 52 83 55 | www.wanhalaamanni.com | Expensive*

WHERE TO STAY

HOTEL SPARRE
A friendly, simply decorated hotel directly in the Old Town with a breakfast terrace. Mon–Fri, sauna incl. *40 rooms | Piispankatu 34 | tel. 019 58 44 55 | Moderate*

TUKKILAN TILA ☺
Farmhouse with Finnhorse stud, steam sauna and organic breakfast, 10 km (6¼ mi) north of the city on the River Porvoo. 27 beds | *Tukkilantie 168, Kerkkoo | tel. 040 5 01 06 39 | www.tukkila.fi | Budget*

INFORMATION

PORVOO TOURIST INFORMATION
Rihkamakatu 4 | tel. 019 5 20 23 16 | www.porvoo.fi

WHERE TO GO

KOTKA (127 D5) (⌀ F13)
In Finland's largest export harbour (pop. 56,000), everything revolves around water, shipping and fish – and the main attractions are related to these. One of the best is the *Maritime Centro Vellamo (Tue–Sun 11am–6pm, Wed until 8pm | 8 euros | Tornatorintie 99 | www.merikeskusvellamo.fi)*. The modern building is in the shape of a huge, gleaming, silver wave. It houses an interactive and contemporary display of items from the collection of Helsinki's former maritime museum. Take a look at the *Kotka Maretarium (mid May–mid Aug daily 10am–8pm, otherwise 10am–5pm | 10 euros | Saponkatu 2 | www.maretarium.fi)*. The aquarium presents Finland's undersea world in 22 themed pools. The highlight is the 7m-high glass wall where you can look salmon, zander and ruffe in the eye. Tourist information office: *Keskuskatu 6 | tel. 05 2 34 44 24 | www.kotka.fi*

LOVIISA (126 C5) (⌀ F13)
The 'pearl of the south coast' is an old garrison town (pop. 16,000; 38 km/23½ mi away) with a beautiful, Neoclassicist centre. Many shops and restaurants are to be found in the wooden house district, and peace and recreation in the wonderful countryside around about. Boats leave from *Laivasilta* for *Svartholm* fortress. Good food and a comfortable bed are to be had in the hotel and restaurant *Degerby (Brandensteininkatu 17 | tel. 019 5 05 61 | www.degerby.com | Moderate)*. Finland's oldest ironworks, *Strömforsin Ruukki*, is a further 15 km (9½ mi) east. It is now a craft village. Tourist information office: *Karlskronabulevardi 8 | www.loviisa.fi*

RASEBORG

(126 B6) (⌀ D14) **Three in one. In 2009, the town Tammisaari was merged with the villages Karis and Pohja to create Raseborg (pop. 30,000) – named after a medieval castle.**
The mild climate, the fascinating coastline and skerries, and the old wooden town of Tammisaari with its beautifully manicured park have made Raseborg one of the most popular areas to spend a holiday in Finland.

SIGHTSEEING

RASEBORG CASTLE

The ruined castle on a rocky outcrop near Snappertuna is unique in the Finnish architectural landscape and a good example of land-rise (post-glacial rebound) – when it was built in the 14th century, the castle was surrounded by the sea. *May–June 10am–5pm, July–mid Aug until 8pm, mid–end Aug until 5pm | free admission*

FISKARS IRONWORKS & VILLAGE ★

Artists and craftspeople now work in the historic buildings in the ironworks near Pohja. They sell designer products, jewellery, glass, works of art made of wood, soap, linen clothing and Fiskars knives. There are cafés and restaurants, exhibitions, museums and paths in the shade of magnificent trees *(Peltorivi 1, Fiskari | www.fiskarsvillage.fi)*. You can stay in the idyllic *B & B Wildrose (3 rooms | Långdalintie 3, Fiskars | tel. 050 5 46 54 87 | www.kolumbus.fi/villiruusu | Moderate)* or in *Wärdshus (15 rooms | Fiskarsintie 14, Fiskars | tel. 019 2 76 65 10 | www.wardshus.fi | Moderate)*.

INSIDER TIP MUSTION LINNA

The 18th-century manor house in the former iron foundry village of Svärt is a remarkable blend of the Rococo and Neoclassical styles, with exquisite parquet floors and Gustavian furnishings, surrounded by a romantic, landscaped garden. The estate is now a museum and park. You can also stay the night in one of the charmingly restored cottages and dine in the first-class restaurant. *Hållsnäsintie 89, Mustio | tel. 019 3 62 31 | www.mustionlinna.fi | Moderate–Expensive*

POJOVIKEN FJORD

Finland's only fjord stretches 15 km (9½ mi) inland from Tammisaari to Skuru. The water flows in two layers, one on top of the other, as the fresh water coming from the streams and rivers is lighter than the salty sea water – a unique feature that has made the fjord an object of research since the beginning of the 20th century. Before you start your tour, stop for your picnic fare at the 🙂 organic farm shop *Mörby Gård* where you can find everything from vegetables to meat. *Mörby Gårds Vägen 80 | tel. 019 20 50 90 | www.morby.fi*

TAMMISAARI

Tammisaari is one of the oldest places in Finland. It received its town charter in 1546 from the Swedish king, Gustav Vasa. The majority of the some 15,000 inhabitants speak Swedish which is why the formerly independent town is often shown as *Ekenäs* on maps.

The well-preserved wooden houses, well-tended parks, a varied coastline and skerries have made this idyllic little coastal town a favourite holiday destination. Thanks to the skerries off shore, the climate here is so mild that even oak trees– a tree seldom found in Finland – grow in and around the town. The Old Town, prettily located on a peninsula, boasts rows of wooden houses with ornately decorated façades. The best view is from the ↘ old water tower on Mill Hill.

The Skerries' National Park lies to the south of the town. This labyrinth of islands, where thousands of seabirds nest in the spring, can only be reached by boat. There are hiking trails on the larger islands *Algö* and *Jussarö*, simple shelters and a barbecue area; on Jussarö there is a café in summer. The pine wood on the western part of this island is a rarity, having remained untouched for centuries. Mini cruises on water taxis take you here, or else go aboard the restaurant ship *M/S Sunnan II (from Norra Hamen north harbour | tel. 019 2 41 18 50 | www.surfnet.fi/saaristoristeilyt)*.

FOOD & DRINK

INSIDER TIP CAFE ADA

Lovely bistro with a view of the north dock in Tammisaari, choice delicacies and good wine. *Daily | Norra Strandgatan 7 | tel. 040 8 01 44 44 | Moderate*

KNIPAN

This, the most popular summer restaurant in Tammisaari, is built on stilts above the sea. Focus on fish and seafood. *June–mid Aug daily, later, until end of Aug, closed Mon/Tue | Strandallén | tel. 019 2 411169 | www.knipan.fi | Moderate*

WHERE TO STAY

FAGERS GÄSTHUS

Here you can stay like the landed gentry in the 18th century. Beautifully restored building in the middle of the Old Town, quiet inner courtyard and friendly hosts. *15 rooms | Rådhustorget, Smedsgatan 6–10, Tammisaari | tel. 0500 44 44 00 | Moderate–Expensive*

HENRIK'S GARDEN ☺

Simple holiday cabin owned by the organic gardeners Henrik and Linnea Landström on the island of Skåldö, 17 km (10½ mi) away. *Sommarövägen 76 | tel. 040 8 20 60 41 | www.henriksgarden.com | Budget*

INFORMATION

RASEBORG TOURIST INFORMATION
Rådhustorget, Tammisaari | tel. 019 2 89 20 10 | www.raseborg.fi

WHERE TO GO

HANKO (126 A6) (𝄐 D14)
The mild climate and 30 km (18½ mi) of fine sandy beach make Hanko the perfect Finnish summer town. Even during the Tsarist era this place was popular – as can be seen by the magnificent, wooden Art Nouveau villas along the waterside promenade. The cliffs on the island of *Hauensuoli,* south of the centre are impressive: over many centuries soldiers and sailors ingraved their names and coat of arms in

Beautiful Finnish Art Nouveau houses: a villa in Hanko

the rock face here. An elegant place to stay is the *Villa Mayja (13 rooms | Appelgrenintie 7 | tel. 050 5 05 20 13 | www.villamaija.fi | Moderate–Expensive)* or, alternatively, in the former police station *(Hotel B8 Bulevardi 8 | 13 rooms | tel. 040 4 85 18 08 | www.hotelb8.fi | Moderate).* Excellent fish is served in *Makasiini (daily | Satamakatu 9 | tel. 019 2 48 40 60 | Moderate).* Tourist information office: *Raatihuoneentori 5 | tel. 019 2 20 34 11 | www.tourism.hanko.fi*

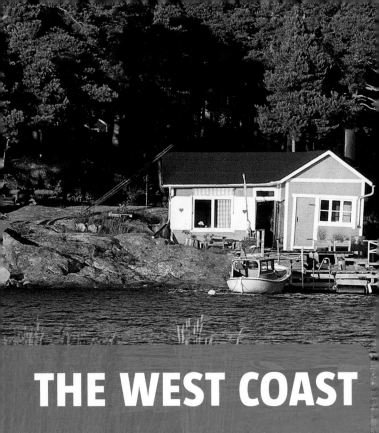

THE WEST COAST

Since the end of the last Ice Age, freed from the massive weight of the ice, new areas of land along the west coast have been rising from the sea. The bays and little islet provide a unique habitat for seabirds, seals and other sea animals – and a popular holiday destination.

That's hardly surprising, as the region boasts not only the most hours of sun in Finland, but also has some of the most beautiful sandy beaches, good fish restaurants and a lot of culture. Finland's oldest towns are on the west coast. Turku, for example, was founded in the 13th century, Rauma and Naantali in the 15th and Pori in the 16th century. In the course of the following 100 years, many other fishing villages and harbours were built, includig the time-honoured towns of Oulu, Vaasa and Uusikaupunki. The flat area inland from the coast is Finland's 'granary' and boasts more than 200 organic farms. Swedish farmhouses, manor houses surrounded by huge fields, woods and wide rivers are typical of this landscape.

ÅLAND

(125 E5) *(∅ B–C 13–14)* ★ **The people here only speak Swedish and yet they belong to Finland. The Åland islands lie**

Photo: The skerries off Rauma

By ferry to the skerries: 6,500 islands
make up the Åland archipelago – boats link
them with one another

between the two Nordic countries in the Gulf of Bothnia.

Sandy beaches and sounds, a mild maritime climate and storm-battered coasts, a rich flora and fauna and omnipresent water characterise the countryside of the 6,500 islands on which there is only one town: *Mariehamn* (125 E5) (ω B14) (pop. 11,000). Founded in 1861, Mariehamn is transformed in summer into a lively little place where people come to enjoy their holidays. The ferry service, that links the largest of the 60 inhabited island with one another, has helped this – and most of the tourists are from Sweden.

Swedish is also the official language of the area. That is the result of political developments in the 20th century: the League of Nations decreed in 1921 that Åland belonged to Finland but that the administra-

Galleon figurehead in Maritime Museum

SIGHTSEEING

ÅLANDS MUSEUM

Focusing on the culture and unsettled history of this island province. *June–Aug daily 10am–5pm, May/Sept/Oct Tue/Thu 10am–8pm, Wed/Fri 10am–4pm, Sat/Sun noon–4pm | 4 euros | Stadshusparken, Mariehamn | www.museum.ax*

ÅLANDS SJÖFARTSMUSEUM (ÅLANDS MARITIME MUSEUM)

Stories about lighthouses, great sailing ships and modern shipping on Åland. Re-opening after renovation after 2012. For opening times, please enquire at museum. *Hamngatan 2, Mariehamn | tel. 018 199 30 | www.sjofartsmuseum.ax*

HILDA HONGELL'S ARCHITECTURE

Of the more than 100 wooden buildings that Finland's first female 'master builder' (1867–1954), 44 are still standing in Mariehamn. The ornamental carving on the buildings at *Södragatan 21* and *Mariegatan 22* is in Swiss style. Other buildings are listed in the *Åland guidebook* available at the tourist information office.

KÄLLSKÄR (125 E5) (*ɯ C14*)

The author of the Moomin stories, Tove Jansson, frequently stayed on this small island south of Kökär. Working from a garden hut. she let herself be inspired by the view and wrote the adventures of these hippo-like mythical creatures. so loved by so many people. Jansson's workplace is now called Moomin House and can be visited together with the Mediterranean garden. *July–beginning of Aug beyond Brudhäll in Karlby, Kökär | 25 euros*

KASTELHOLMS SLOTT ★ (125 E5) (*ɯ B13*)

This castle from the 14th century is the most-visited attraction on Åland. In its

tion of its affairs would lie in its own hands. The predominant language resulted from the islands being part of Sweden for centuries. As a symbol of its unique status, Åland also has its own flag and its own stamps. Since 1854, the region is a demilitarised zone thanks to the Åland Convention.

Visitors can reach the island group by plane or ship from Helsinki, Turku, Stockholm and Tallinn. Journeys by ship can be booked on the *Eckerö Linjen, Tallink Silja* or *Viking Lines*. Alternatively, you can take a local ferry along the north route from Ösnäs or along the south route from Galtby. Cars have to be booked in advance with the ferry services: *tel. Mon–Sat 9am–5pm, June/July Mon–Fri 8am–5pm, Sat 9am–3pm | tel. 018 52 51 00 | www.alandstrafiken.ax*

THE WEST COAST

heyday in the 15th and 16th centuries, it was the base of the Swedish crown. After plundering and a series of fires, the ruins revealed very little left of its former glory. However, for more than 30 years now, efforts have been made to rebuild the castle which, surrounded by a moat, rises picturesquely above the surrounding countryside. Attached to it are the *Vita Björn Prison Museum* and the *Jan Karlsgården Farmhouse Museum.* ● The midsummer celebrations here are colourful: the St John's Day tree is traditionally decorated and the dancing and singing go on deep into the night. In mid July, the *Gustav Vasa Days* are held around Kastelholm when there is also a medieval market. *July daily 10am–6pm, May/June as well as Aug–15 Sept 10am–5pm | 5 euros | Sund | www.museum.ax*

CHURCHES

There are twelve medieval fieldstone churches on Åland with beautiful towers. The church in *Jomala* from 1270 is the old-est stone building in Finland. The church in *Finström* has precious frescoes, painted directly on plaster using the secco technique. The other churches are in *Eckerö, Föglö, Geta, Hammarland, Kumlinge, Lemland, Saltvik, Sund* and on *Vardö* – the name of the latter meaning 'look-out island'. It is a reminder of times long ago when Vardö was a stop-over on the mail route from Turku to Stockholm

POMMERN MUSEUM SHIP

The last four-master in the world still in its original condition is docked in the west harbour in Mariehamn. The 'queen of sailing ships' was built in 1903 and used to transport grain between Australia, England and Denmark. It was taken out of service in 1939. Since 1953 the Pommern has been as museum ship. A highly recommendable exhibition is on board as well as a documentary film on life at sea. *May, June and Aug daily 9am–5pm, July daily 9am–7pm, Sept daily 10am–4pm | 5 euros | www.mariehamn.ax/pommern*

MARCO POLO HIGHLIGHTS

⭐ **Åland islands**
Pearls between Finland and Sweden: the archipelago of the south-west coast comprises 6,500 islands → p. 50

⭐ **Kastelholms Slott**
Once home to the powerful kings of Sweden → p. 52

⭐ **Kvarken Archipelago**
This is where new land is gradually rising from the sea → p. 58

⭐ **Turun Linna Castle**
The oldest medieval castle in Finland has a chequered history → p. 61

⭐ **Luostarinmäki Craft Museum**
The unique historical district of Turku provides a perfect setting for this museum in which ancient crafts have been brought back to life in 30 workshops → p. 61

⭐ **Naantali**
The town is washed by the sea on three sides, yachts are anchored in the marina and Art Nouveau villas line the sea promenade → p. 62

⭐ **Rauma**
The most extensive, historical wooden town in Scandinavia is now a World Heritage Site → p. 63

ÅLAND

ECKERÖ POST & CUSTOMS HOUSE
(125 E5) (*ØØ B13*)

This imposing Neoclassical building is a reminder of the old mail route between Stockholm and St Petersburg. Inside are a post office, a museum, the *Formriket* craft studio and several galleries. *(June–15 Aug daily 10am–3pm, 16 June–31 July until 4pm).* The handmade chocolates sold in the *Lugn och Ro* café make nice souvenirs. *May–Aug daily 10am–4pm, July until 6pm | Sandmovägen, Storby, Eckerö | tel. 018 3 84 20*

MARIEHAMN SJÖKVARTERET
(SEAFARING DISTRICT)

The smell of tar lies in the air: the seafarers's world comes alive in the east harbour *(Österleden)* in Mariehamn. If they are not at sea, three-master and other sailing ships are moored up against the quay. There is a small shipyard with a forge and boat museum *(mid June–mid Aug daily 10am–6pm, otherwise Mon–Fri 9am–11am) | 4 euros).* The *Salt Craftsmen's House (Mon–Fri 10am–5pm, Sat 10am–* 2pm, July–mid Aug Mon–Fri until 6pm, Sat until 3pm, Sun noon–3pm)* and the vegetarian ☺ *Café Bönan (June–Aug daily 10.30am–6pm)* are also in this district.

FOOD & DRINK

Apart from fresh fish of all varieties, typical delicacies from Åland include sweet rye bread, buckthorn products, cheese as well as Åland pancakes. *Stallhagen beer*, available in many places, comes from Åland's brewery whereas the *Tjudö* distillery produces liqueurs and rum *(for information and guided tours see: www.visitaland.com/tjudovingard).* A white wave on a blue background is the symbol for the ☺ *skerries' 'Good Taste' seal of approval* issued by a network of companies that produces and sells local produce.

ÅSS PAVILJON

The favourite summer restaurant in Mariehamn is directly on the marina. Located in a wooden building, Michael Björklund's crew serves an early summer, midsummer

If you paddle to Kobba Klintar by kajak, you will see the old and new pilots' houses from far off

and late summer menu with fresh ingredients from Åland for the more demanding clientele, as well as snacks and wines. *May–Sept daily | beach promenade | tel. 018 19 14 1 | Moderate–Expensive*

BAGARSTUGAN CAFÉ & VIN
Reliable and good restaurant and café open for lunches, in a lovely, old wooden house with small, intimate rooms and a summer terrace. *Closed Sun | Ekonomiegatan 2, Mariehamn | tel. 018 198 80 | Moderate*

DEGERBY MAT & CAFÉ
Daily lunch menu and à la carte during the high season; unpretentious regional cooking with a café. Rooms with breakfast. *Tingsvägen 7, Föglö | tel. 018 5 00 02 | Moderate*

RESTAURANT Q ☺
Meat from naturally reared animals and regional produce are used to conjure up dishes inspired by the Mediterranean. Lovely terrace with a view of the sandy

beach, cliffs and trees exposed to the wind. *June–Aug daily | Eckerö | tel. 018 3 80 04 | Budget*

INSIDER TIP SOLTUNA ☼
Light dishes and snacks in the café or classical, high-quality fish and meat specialities in the restaurant. Good sea views from the terrace and tower. A footpath from here leads to some caves. *Mid April–mid Sept daily | Västergeta, Geta | tel. 018 4 95 30 | Budget–Moderate*

SPORTS & ACTIVITIES

Equipment and training can be found on the islands for almost any conceivable sport, from bike rental, kajak and boat hire, para-sailing, kite-surfing or diving. Beach volleyball, tennis and riding as well as guided fishing trips and seal safaris are on offer.

BOAT OUTINGS
Tours to the old ship pilots' houses on the island of *Kobba Klintar* are popular, either with a motorboat from Korrvik marina in Mariehamn *(early July–mid Aug daily, until end of Sept Fri–Sun 11am)* or in an organised paddle tour *(June–Aug Sat 11am–5pm | tel. 018 14757 | www.sgu.nu)*

BEACHES, POOLS & SAUNAS
There are more than 30 officially listed sandy beaches in Åland, the nicest ones being on Eckerö – namely *Degersand, Käringssund* and *Sandviken*. By bad weather, *Mariebad (Mon noon–10pm, Tue–Fri 10am–10pm Sat/Sun 10am–6pm | entrance fee from 4.60 euros | Österleden)* near the Mariehamn seafaring district is a good place to go. A ● INSIDER TIP ▶ visit to a floating sauna is an experience not to be forgotten: Sandösund campsite on Vårdö has built its saunas on pontoons and moored them in the lake *(www.sandosund.com)*

WHERE TO STAY

BASTÖ HOTELL & STUGBY
Holiday resort with hotel, cabins and beach sauna, centrally situated on the main island. *20 rooms, 20 cabins | May–Sept | Pålsböle, Finström | tel. 018 4 23 82 | www.basto.ax | Moderate*

BRUDHÄLL HOTELL & RESTAURANG
The interlocking wooden building built like a collection of boathouses, is idyllically located in a bay on Kökar. Excellent cuisine with regional ingredients and huge sailors' breakfast. *19 rooms | Karlby, Kökar | tel. 018 5 59 55 | www.brudhall.com | Moderate*

HAVSVIDDEN HOTEL AND RESORT
This spa hotel is on a peninsula on the island of Geta. There is a good speciality restaurant, a smoke sauna on the beach, spa, swimming pool and many rooms with a lovely view (justa ask!). *33 rooms | Havsviddsvägen 90, Geta | tel. 018 49 40 8 | www.havsvidden.com | Moderate–Expensive*

NYBONDS PENSIONAT 😊
More like home than a guesthouse. This old captain's house with its pretty traditional garden has been carefully renovated. If you like, you can join courses (yoga, watercolour painting, etc.). The cooking is with regional and organic produce and bedlinen for allergy sufferers is also available. *3 rooms | Kolsvidjavägen 291, Tranvik, Sund | tel. 040 5 87 95 56 | www.visitaland.com/nybondspensionat/de | Budget*

INSIDER TIP SVISKÄR
De luxe living for hermits: a holiday home that sleeps four – who get on well with each other – can be rented on the island of Sviskär. There's no electricity but instead no limit to the natural surroundings or amount of cosiness. Mobile phones can be deposited at the jetty on arrival. If required, full board is possible in the form of a picnic hamper from the up-market restaurant on the main island Silverskär. *To the north, opposite Saltvik | tel. 018 52 55 65 | www.visitaland.com/silverskar/en | Expensive*

INFORMATION

MARIEHAMN TOURIST INFORMATION
Storagatan 8 | tel. 018 2 40 00 | www.visitaland.com

ÖSTERBOTTEN

The stretch of land between Kristiinankaupunki and Oulu is blessed by the sun. This has given rise to a popular tourist route along the coast being called the 'Sun Route' which leads from the southwest up to Oulu.

LOW BUDGET

▶ The *Åland ferries* offer cheaper fares to those who spend a night on their way to and from the harbour at the end of the archipelago. ● Yellow ferries are generally free. Information: *www.alandstrafiken.ax*

▶ Free admission is also given to the beautifully located *Jan Karlsgården Open-Air Museum*. The pretty museum includes demonstrations of traditional crafts. *May–Sept daily 10am–5pm | Kastelholm, Mariehamn*

▶ The youth hostel in Turku is one of the best in Finland. *23 rooms | spacious doubles 45 euros, dormitory 18 euros per person | Linnankatu 39 | tel. 02 2 62 76 80 | www.turku.fi/hostelturku*

The route takes you through fishing villages and harbour towns that are among the oldest in Finland. Further inland, the flat countryside of this area of East Bothnia, where cereals and vegetables are grown, is broken up by pastureland and fields of crops, glasshouses and farms and countless, large rivers – full of fish – which flow into the sea. Everywhere here is strongly influenced by Sweden and both languages are spoken. The region, Ostrobothnia in English, is known as *Österbotten* in Swedish and *Pohjanmaa* in Finnish.

SIGHTSEEING

INSIDER TIP ▶ ARCHIPELAGO OF THE SEVEN BRIDGES (122 B5) (*⒨ D9*)

This 40 km (25 mi) stretch of the Sun Route is one of the most beautiful: the coastal road no. 749 leads over seven bridges through the skerries of *Jakobstad Pietarsaari* (pop. 20,000) to *Kokkola* (pop. 46,000). Both towns are well known for their listed wooden house districts.

Have a look around and visit the *Nanoq Arctic Museum* in Jakobstad, a peat house built in the traditional Greenland manner *(June–Aug daily noon–6pm | 7 euros | Pörkenäsintie 60 | www.nanoq.fi)* and just soak up the atmosphere of the seascape. On the lighthouse island of *Tankar* you can daydream before tucking in to a fish soup and spending the night there *(ferries 3 times a day | www.tourismkokkola.fi, www.tankar.fi).*

KALAJOKI ● (128 C4) (*⒨ D9*)

The longest sandy beach in Finland is the main summer attraction that this little town (pop. 13,000) has to offer. The dance pavilion *Merisärkkä* – right on the beach *(Sat | Pakkainpolku 20 | www.merisarkka. fi)* – is also popular. From May until October ferries operate to the autonomous fishing islands of *Maakalla* and *Ulkokalla* that rose

Land ahoy: on the ferry to the Åland islands

from the sea in the 15th century *(4-hour trip for 58 euros per person | www.feme mare.fi).*

KRISTIINANKAUPUNKI (125 F2) (*⒨ C11*)

Narrow lanes, romantic fountains and a lovely wooden church make this wooden town (pop. 7000) so idyllic. The *Wolf's Cave* nearby towards Karijoki was inhabited in the Stone Age. Tools that are more than 120,000 years old were found in a cravasse. Access to Wolf's Cave has been blocked now for some years but there is a information centre with a café *(June/ July daily, Aug Mon–Fri 11am–5.30pm | free admission | Paarmanninvuori | www. susiluola.fi).*

INSIDER TIP ▶ SJÖDERFARDEN
(125 F1) (*CD C10*)

Created by a meteorite 520 million years ago, this perfectly round area (almost 9 mi²) is an important resting place for migrating cranes. A visitors' centre nearby (road no. 673 via Maalahti) has a look-out and space telescope *(mid May–end Sept Wed 4pm–8pm, Sun 2pm–8pm | 4 euros | www.meteoria.fi).*

VAASA (125 F1) (*CD C10*)

The town (pop. 59,000) is the centre of the region of Ostrobothnia. The university town was founded in 1606 and was burnt to the ground all too often in subsequent centuries. Rebuilding often resulted in a number of eye-sores – and present-day Vaasa is not known for its beauty. Nevertheless it is visited by lots of tourist. One reason for this is its strategic position for breaking the journey from Turku to Oulu. The second and more important reason lies off shore. This is where the ★ *Kvarken Archipelago* is located – a geological wonderland that is now a Unesco World Heritage Site. Every year the land rises by about one centimetre. New islands emerge and cliffs grow out of the water. Boathouses that were once on the water now find themselves high and dry after several years. The reason behind this phenomenon: so-called glacio-isostatic uplift. Nowhere else in the world can the effect of this be seen so clearly as here. Info: *Terranova Kvarken Nature Centre (Tue/Thu/Fri 10am–5pm, Wed until 8pm, Sat/Sun noon–5pm | Museokatu 3 | 5 euros | terranova.vaasa.fi*

If you would like to stay on, try the stylishly furnished *Hotel Kantarellis* in the town centre, all 58 rooms have their own sauna *(Rosteeninkatu 6 | tel. 06 3 57 81 00 | www.hotelkantarellis.fi | Moderate).* Tourist information office: *Raastuvankatu 30 | tel. 06 3 25 11 45 | matkailu.vaasa.fi*

OULU

(128 D3) (*CD E8*) **With a hint of a large city: before heading further northwards into the lonliness of Lapland, you can sample urban life one last time in Oulu.**
By Finnish standards, the privincial capital exudes something of the air of a major city – after all, almost 140,000 people live here. The town has existed for more than 400 years, developing as the centre of an ancient industry: trading with tar. In the 18th and 19th centuries Oulu was the biggest export harbour for tar in the world. The tar boat rowing race in June *(www.tervasoutu.fi)* and the tar bonfire on midsummer's day are reminders of this time. After a major fire in 1822, Oulu was rebuilt in the Neoclassicist style. Today, the town is a pleasant mixture of modern and traditional things in a lovely setting at the Oulujoki estuary, with a wide range of cultural events, good shops and 250 miles of cycle paths.

SIGHTSEEING

TUOMIOKIRKKO (CATHEDRAL)
The 56m-high (184 ft) bell-tower of this Neoclassicist church is a symbol of the town and rose from the ashes in a completely new style after the massive fire of 1832. *June–Aug daily 11am–9pm | corner of Kirkkokatu/Asemakatu 6*

KAUPPATORI (MARKET SQUARE)
An Art Nouveau market hall, restored salt storehouses and market stalls make up the heart of the town, with the statue of the little market sheriff *toripoliisi* keeping an eye on what is going on. From here, the Old Town with its pedestrianised roads and many shops, cafés and department stores is no distance, and bridges lead to other districts of the town.

POHJOIS-POHJANMAAN MUSEO (NORTHERN OSTROBOTHNIA MUSEUM)

The region's archeological treasures are exhibited on four floors in this museum together with displays from the world of manufacturing and everyday items from different periods, as well as a comprehensive collection on the Sami culture. *Tue–Sun 10am–5pm, early June–mid Aug Fri 10am–6pm, Sat/Sun 11am–6pm | 3 euros | Ainolan Puisto | www.ouka.fi/ppm*

TIETOMAA SCIENCE CENTRE

This award-winning museum explains scientific, natural and technical things in an entertaining way. More than 170 hands-on exhibits with which to experiment. With a cinema, café and ⚓ tower with a wonderful view. *Daily 10am–5pm, seasonal variations | 15 euros | Nahkatehtaankatu 6 | www.tietomaa.fi*

HELLA

This little restaurant magically transforms fresh ingredients including fish and venison with dates and orange sauce into unbe-known tasty treats. Specialities include steaks, duck's liver tortellini and chocolate cake. Good wines. *Daily. | Isokatu 13 | tel. 08 37 11 80 | Moderate–Expensive*

PUISTOLA

Deli, bistro and restaurant in the renovated Puistola Art Nouveau building. Good value for money in the mornings, expensive in the evenings: breakfast from 7.30am *(Budget)*, light lunches in the bistro *(daily | Moderate)* and salads in the deli *(Mon–Sat | Moderate)*, haute-cuisine in the restaurant in the evening *(closed Sun/Mon | Expensive)*. *Pakkahuonekatu 15 | tel. 020 7 92 82 10 | www.ravintolapuistola.fi*

Off for a stroll around the town: in summer life in Oulu revolves around the market square

SOKERI-JUSSIN KIEVARI
Traditional Finnish dishes such as elk steak in an old wooden storehouse on *Pikisaari* Island. The ice cream served on the summer terrace is also traditional in flavour – one even tastes of tar. *Daily | Pikisaarentie 2 | tel. 08 37 66 28 | Expensive*

SPORTS & ACTIVITIES

OULUN EDEN HOLIDAY CLUB ●
(128 C3) *(𝓂 E8)*
This spa is located on the sandy beach on Hietasaari Island, with a wonderful view of the sea. Tropical swimming pool, Finnish and Turkish saunas, massages, aromatherapy and cosmetic treatment. The spa is attached to a hotel but can also be visited by non-residents. *Daily 10am–9pm | 15 euros | tel. 020 123 49 05 | Holstinsalmentie 29 | www.holidayclubspahotels.com*

WHERE TO STAY

LASARETTI
This elegant hotel lies concealed behind a red-brick façade. The Lasaretti is centrally located in the municipal park *Hupisaaret*, with the rooms overlooking the estuary. Sauna, swimming pool and gym. *49 rooms | Kasarmintie 13 | tel. 020 7 57 47 00 | www.lasaretti.com | Expensive*

RADISSON BLU
Good, comfortable hotel right on the market square, with spacious rooms overlooking the sea or the river. Friendly staff, bright breakfast room. *221 rooms | Hallituskatu 1 | tel. 020 123 47 00 | www.radissonblu.com/hotel-oulu | Moderate–Expensive*

INFORMATION

OULU TOURIST INFORMATION
Torikatu 10 | tel. 044 7 03 13 30 | www.visitoulu.fi

WHERE TO GO

TURKANSAARI OPEN-AIR MUSEUM
(129 D3) *(𝓂 E8)*
The traditions of the farming, woodcutting and tar working communities of old are brought back to life in the 40 buildings reerected here. Access is by river steamer. *End May–mid Aug daily 10am–6pm, until mid Sept 10am–4pm | 3 euros | www.ouka.fi/ppm/turkansaari*

LIMINGANLAHTI (128 C4) *(𝓂 E8)*
This bay is a paradise for ornithologists. Liminganlahti is Finland's most precious wetland area. Many rare breeds of bird such as harriers, owls and willow grouse live amongst the reeds and birches. A nature conservation centre, a good network of boardwalks and five observation hides facilitate bird watching *(www.limingan lahti.fi).*

TURKU

(124 C4) *(𝓂 D13)* **The charming and lively university town of Turku – or Åbo in Swedish – surrounded by islands and skerries, spreads out in all directions.**
Under Swedish rule, Turku was the capital of Finland and the country's major commercial centre until 1812. It was the Russian Tsar who moved the capital to Helsinki, to be closer to St Petersburg. Turku was ravaged by a fire in 1827 which destroyed three quarters of the town and lost its university and supremecy. Nevertheless, many Finns considered this town (pop. 176,000), with its episcopal see and long shipbuilding tradition, to be the cultural capital. Turku is divided into two by the River Aura, is bi-lingual and blessed with historical and cultural treasures and a picturesque coastline dotted with skerries. Ferry links connect it with Åland, Sweden and Tallinn.

SIGHTSEEING

ABOA VETUS AND ARS NOVA

The ruins for the monastic distric Aboa Vetus (14th century) were discovered by chance when building the Museum of Modern Art (Ars Nova) and integrated in the design. *April–mid Sept daily 11am–7pm, otherwise closed Mon | 8 euros | Itäinen Rantakatu 4–6 | www.aboavetusarsnova.fi*

TURUN LINNA (CASTLE) ⭐

The town's first place of interest welcomes visitors when the arrive at the ferry terminal in the harbour. The oldest medieval castle in the coutries stands facing you, defiant and grey. It was built in 1280 and slighted and remodelled time and again before finally being restored in 1980 into its imposing present state. It now houses the Historical Museum. Exhibitions and concerts are regularly held here. *In summer Tue–Sun 10am–6pm, end Sept–end April Wed only noon–8pm | 7 euros | Linnankatu 80 | www.turku.fi/museo*

TUOMIOKIRKKO (CATHEDRAL)

Finnish national sanctuary from the 13th century and the principal church of the Lutherian congregation. The simple, severe lines of the Neoclassicist style characterise this building from 1832. *Daily 9am–7pm, in summer until 8pm | 2 euros | Tuomiokirkonkatu 1*

FORUM MARINUM

Maritime centre with an impressive fleet of museum ships. Pikkuföri ferry terminal for trips up the river and around the harbour. *Museum: Oct–April Tue–Sun 11am–6pm, May–Sept 11am–7pm | 7 euros | Linnankatu 72 | www.forum-marinum.fi; ships: June–Aug 11am–7pm | day pass 12 euros*

LUOSTARINMÄKI CRAFT MUSEUM ⭐ ●

In summer, weavers, carpenters and wood turners populate the 30 craft workshops. You can watch, take part or buy finished items in the shop. *May–Sept Tue–Sun 10am–6pm | 6 euros | Vartiovuorenkatu 2*

Ships for tours around the skerries leave regularly from Turku harbour

FOOD & DRINK

CINDY LAIVARAVINTOLA

Floating restaurant in a converted barge with traditional Finnish food. Large terrace on the upper deck welcomes guests in summer. *Daily | Itäinen Rantakatu, at Theatre Bridge | tel. 010 2 31 01 80 | Moderate*

MAMI

This 'in' restaurant is a typical representative of modern, Finnish cooking. There are not many dishes to choose from on the menu but they are exquisite. Lovely location on the River Aura. *Closed Sun/Mon | Linnankatu 3 | tel. 02 2 311111 | www.mami. fi | Moderate*

SPORTS & ACTIVITIES

DRAISINE RIDE

A trip into the surrounding countryside for the active can be had on a hand-operated rail-cycle – a Draisine – (for 1–6 people) on the disused track from Kankaanpää via Pomarkku and Noormarkku to Pori. If the 48 km (30 mi) tour is too much on the arms, shorter distances are also possible. 4 hours cost 10 euros, a day's outing 20 euros. Information and reservation: *Antti Mäkinen | tel. 02 6 4152 52 or 0500 32 35 36 | www.pomarkku.fi*
In Noormarkku you can also visit the Villa Mayrea designed by Alvar Aalto if you book in advance. *Laviantie 4, Noormarkku | tel. 010 8 88 44 60 | www.villamairea.fi*

RUISSALO

To the south-west of Turku is the island Ruissalo, connected to the mainland by a bridge. Covering just 3 mi², the island is now a place of recreation where you can cycle, play golf and walk. To the south there is a beach with impressive villas along the shore. In mid-July the birds in the nearby sanctuary get a shock three days long. That is when *Ruisrock*, Finland's most famous rock festival takes place and 90,000 people squeeze themselves onto tiny Ruissalo *(www.ruisrock.fi)*.

ENTERTAINMENT

INSIDER TIP VALASRANTA DANCE PAVILION

Waltz and tango, humppa and foxtrot: the dance pavilion in Yläne puts everyone in party mood along the lakeside. An ur-Finnish experience. *Sat (in summer also Tue/Thu) | Valasrannantie 363 | bus from Turku bus station | www.valasranta.fi*

WHERE TO STAY

PARK HOTEL

Peacefully located, Art Nouveau hotel on Puolala Park and not far from the station. Individually furnished rooms, friendly service. *21 rooms | Rauhankatu 1 | tel. 02 2 73 25 55 | www.parkhotelturku.fi | Expensive*

TUURE BED & BREAKFAST

Overnight stays in a commercial building with no frills, friendly service, pet cat, free Internet, conveniently and centally situated. *15 rooms | Tuureporinkatu 17C | tel. 02 2 33 02 30 | www.tuure.fi | Budget*

INFORMATION

TURKU TOURING

Aurakatu 4 | 02 2 62 74 44 | www.turku touring.fi

WHERE TO GO

NAANTALI ⭐ (124 B4) (ﾑ C13)

If you want to arrive in style, come by steamer. This little town (pop. 19,000) is a favourite stop-over for people on their way north. In summer, the *M/S Ukkopekka*, the last operating steamer in the skerries,

Wooden houses and a maritime atmosphere characterise the spa town of Naantali

completes the trip from Turku to Naantali in just under 2 hours (www.ukkopekka.fi). On land, the traditional Finnish summer resort awaits you with its wooden villas, spa and lively sea promenade. Apart from the Old Town and the convent church from 1462, Moominworld (see section: 'Travel with Kids') and the summer residence of the Finnish President, *Kultaranta*, are well-worth seeing. INSIDER TIP Kultaranta park is a mini, northern version of Versailles, where 3500 rosebushes flower in the summer. The residence is on Luonnonmaa Island, connected to the mainland by a bridge (guided tours from end of June–mid Aug 2pm/3pm | 10 euros). Tourist information office: tel. 02 4 35 98 00 | www.naantalinmatkailu.fi/eng

RAUMA ★ (124 A1) (*ℳ C12*)

Plan some time for a walk. The historical ensemble of this town (pop. 40,000), some 90 km (56 mi) away, is an artwork to be marvelled at. Rauma's narrow alleyways and 200 little shops invite you to browse. The 600 wooden houses in the Old Town, which are still lived in to-day, are a World Heritage Site (www.old rauma.fi).

In addition to its beautiful buildings, Rauma is widely known for lacemaking. At the end of July, the lacemakers – masters of their craft – exhibit their hand-made products at the traditional Lace Week. The highlight of this festival is the Black Lace Night on Friday. If you want to stay a bit longer, how about combining the charm of the town with the flair of the coast – and choose somewhere to sleep a little out of town? The island *Kylmäpihlaja* can be reached from Rauma every day in summer (June–Aug). The lighthouse is now a hotel and restaurant with expansive views over the open sea (11 rooms | tel. 044 0 82 29 64 | www.kylmapihlaja.com | *Moderate*). Tourist information office: changing locations | tel. 02 8 34 35 12 | www.visitrauma.fi

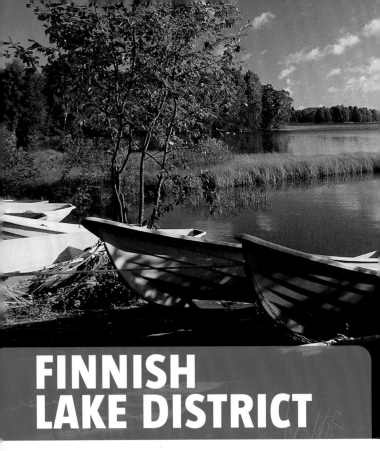

FINNISH LAKE DISTRICT

Finland's reputation as the 'country of thousands of lakes' is due to the some 40,000 stretches of water in the Finnish Lake District. The region between Jyväskylä and Tampere in the west, and Savonlinna and Lappeenranta in the east, is a unique blend of water, hills and woods. This patchwork of blues and greens is a magical, unpolluted natural environment. The lakes *Saimaa* and *Päijänne* are the largest and cleanest bodies of water in Europe. In between, there are headlands and ridges, including the well-known, nationally important landscape around Punkaharju. In this area you can experience Finland as if in a picture book.

JYVÄSKYLÄ

(126 C2) (*DI E11*) The capital of Central Finland (pop. 130,000) should really be called Alvar Aalto Town. This is where the Finnish architect launched his career and 30 of his buildings have given Jyväskyla its characteristic appearance.

If you're looking for romantic wooden buildings, you'll be searching in vain. But if you're a fan of classical modern architecture, you'll want to spend some time in this town. Whether it is the university, the municipal theatre or the police station – many public buildings were designed by

Photo: On the bank of Lake Päijänne

Perfect days at the lake: rowing boats and summer houses await holiday-makers to Lake Saimaa and Lake Päijänne

Alvar Aalto. The *architectural site map* available for 2 euros from the tourist information office will give put you in the picture.

SIGHTSEEING

ALVAR AALTO MUSEUM

At the town's request, Aalto erected a monument to his own work with this building. Sketches and photos, designer objects, models and furniture provide an insight into his life. *Tue–Sun 11am–6pm | 6 euros | Alvar Aallonkatu 7 | www.alvaraalto.fi*

CRAFT MUSEUM

Felt work, carving, plaiting: traditional Finnish crafts are as alive today as 100 years ago. You can even make your own souvenir in the museum craft studios or buy something made by one of the professionals

A hiker's paradise: Isojärvi National Park

in the museum shop. *Tue–Sun 11am–6pm | 6 euros | Kauppakatu 25 | www.craft museum.fi*

ART MUSEUM AND CENTRE FOR PRINTMAKING

Finnish and international contemporary art, modern prints and creative photography in two buildings. *Tue–Sun 11am–6pm | Taidemuseo Holvi (art museum): Kauppakatu 23; Grafiikkakeskus (centre for printmaking): 6 euros | Hannikaisenkatu 39 | www.jyvaskyla.fi/taidemuseo*

FOOD & DRINK

INSIDERTIP KISSANVIIKSET

This small elegant restaurant has been conjuring up perfectly balance Finnish meat and fish delicacies and seasonal specialities for more than 40 years. *Daily | Puistokatu 3 | tel. 010 6 66 51 50 | www. kissanviikset.fi | Moderate*

MUMMON PULLAPUOTI

Café in the *Forum* shopping centre with a large selection of *pulla*, sweet Finnish cardamom bread. *Closed Sun | Asemakatu 7*

OLD BRICKS INN

Nostalgic pub with a good selection of beer and food. The terrace is normally full on sunny evenings. *Daily | Kauppakatu 41 | tel. 014 61 62 33 | Moderate*

SOPPABAARI

Cheap and imaginatively prepared soups, noodle and vegetarian dishes. *Closed Sun | Väinönkatu 26 | tel. 014 4 49 80 01 | Budget*

SHOPPING

Individual and natural linen fashions can be found at *Pellava-Akka (Tue–Thu | Kauppakatu 5)* and *Pellavainen (Mon–Fri | Kauppakatu 4)*. Beautiful turned-wood and enamel artworks is sold in the *Satamakapteeni restaurant* in Korpilahti harbour *(daily | Korpilahdentie | www.satamakapteeni.fi)*.

SPORTS & ACTIVITIES

All sorts of leisure activities are concentrated around *Lake Jyväsjärvi*. The tourist information office can provide addresses for bike hire, water sports, golf, riding or hot-air balloon rides. The 12 km (7½ mi) *Rantaraitt path* takes you around the lake. If you just want to stroll, the little town park, *Harju,* is perfect. A good view of the town and lake can be had in the ☕ café in the *Vesilinna water tower.*

WHERE TO STAY

KAMPUS

Simple guesthouse near the university, in-room cooking facilities and fridge. *9 rooms | Kauppakatu 11A | tel. 014 3 38 14 00 | www. kolumbus.fi/pensionkampus | Budget*

FINNISH LAKE DISTRICT

TAULUN KARTANO ☺

Pure nostalgia: this historic manorial farm (35 km/22 mi away) has been carefully restored. The rooms are romantic; the cooking with regional organic produce; Iceland ponies are ready for a ride. Apart from 16 rooms, typically Finnish wooden cabins are available for rent; 1070 ft² log cabin sauna on *Pieni Kankainen* lake. *Tauluntie 596, Kankainen | tel. 044 0 88 45 90 | www.taulunkartano.fi | Moderate*

HOTEL YÖPUU

Small, intimate hotel in one of the few older buildings in the town. Gourmet standard cuisine served in the restaurants *Pöllöwaari* and *Ranskalaiset Korot*. *26 rooms | Yliopistonkatu 23 | tel. 014 33 39 00 | www.hotelliyopuu.fi | Moderate*

INFORMATION

JYVÄSKYLÄ TOURIST INFORMATION
Asemakatu 6 | tel. 014 2 66 01 13 | www.jyvaskylanseutu.fi

WHERE TO GO

JÄMSÄ (126 C3) (*ΩΩ E12*)

This town (pop. 23,000), 58 km (36 mi) away, on the west shore of *Lake Päijänne*, is the home of felt-making. Products, such as slippers and hats made of this sheer indestructible material, can be bought from two factory outlets: *Alhon Huopatehdas Oy (Partalantie 131)* and *Huopaliike Lahtinen Ay (Partalantie 267)*. The Himos hills and the Isojärvi National Park are popular hiking areas, and various day-tours (20–40 euros) around the lake leave from the harbour *(www.paijannematkat.com)*.

INSIDER TIP ▶ MÄNTTÄ (126 C3) (*ΩΩ E11*)

Art always played a special role in the lives of the old, Finnish, entrepreneurial Serlachius family. The patriarch, Gustav Adolf, started a collection a hundred years ago that was continued and expanded by his nephew, Gösta. One of the largest art foundations in northern Europe emerged as a result. It supports two museums: while *Gösta* (housed in a manorial farm) is devoted to art, *Gustav* (in the former Serlachius company headquarters) focuses on Finnish history and tales – including that of the paper factory in Mänttä where everything began. *June–Aug Tue–Sun 11am–6pm, Sept–May Wed 2pm–8pm, Thu–Sun noon–5pm | 8 euros | www.serlachius.fi*

MUURAME ● (126 C3) (*ΩΩ E11*)

Sweating in the time-honoured way: the village (pop. 9000) has an *Open-Air Sauna Museum,* with some 30 old and new saunas from all over Finland. The oldest model dates from the 17th century. You can try things out too: every Wednesday there is a smoke sauna evening *(6pm–8pm)*. *June–Aug Tue–Sun 10am–5pm | Mertamäentie | 5 euros | www.muurame.fi/saunakyla*

MARCO POLO HIGHLIGHTS

⭐ **Päijänne**
The pearl of the Finnish lake district → p. 68

⭐ **Saimaa lake district**
14,000 islands and its own species of seal → p. 69

⭐ **Olavinlinna Castle**
The medieval castle in Savonlinna is the background for the opera festival every year → p. 73

⭐ **Punkaharju**
A captivatingly beautiful headland in a blue-green painting of water and woodland → p. 75

INSIDER TIP **PETÄJÄVESI**
(126 C2) (*E11*)

This village (pop. 4000) some 35 km (22 mi) west of Jyväskylä is famous for its old wooden church. This lovely building (*Vanhankirkontie 9*) from 1764 is an exceptional example of Finnish carpentry and is a World Heritage Site *(June–Aug daily 10am–6pm, service Sun 10am | 5 euros)*. *Heinähattu* in the village sells 🕐 organic and regional produce (*Kirkkotie 3*).

PÄIJÄNNE ★ (126 C2–4) (*E12*)

Finland's second largest lake stretches for 119 km (74 mi) – including its arms – as far as Lahti. It supplies drinking water for more than 1 million people, that goes to speak for its purity. It does not come without reason that it is called the 'pearl of the Finnish lake district'. Some 1900 island are scattered across this huge body of water. A two-day boat trip from Jyväskylä to Lahti with lots of stops on the way, takes you through lakeland scenery in which many Finns have a *mökki* close to the banks of the lake – a privilege from times past. Nowadays, new summerhouses in Finland can only be built a minimum distance from the water. *Mid June– mid Aug | Tue from Lahti, Wed from Jyväskylä | 100 euros per person incl. hotel | www.paijanne-risteilythilden.fi*

LAPPEEN-RANTA

(127 E4) (*G12*) **This town with a population of 72,000 is the southern starting point for tours across Lake Saimaa. In the Middle Ages it was a trading station and received a town charter from Queen Cristina I of Sweden in 1649.**

Today, Lappeenranta is an important centre for trade with Russia thanks to the 43 km-long (27 mi) Saimaa Canal, and is Finland's most important inland port. The lively

Nothing but blues and greens: an afternoon on Lake Päijänne

harbour promenade flanked by lime trees, the historic buildings, the 13,000 students and the warm-hearted South Karelian lifestyle give this town its charming character.

SIGHTSEEING

LINNOITUS (FORTRESS DISTRICT)

This historic district is situated on a headland near the harbour and includes the now overgrown ruins of the old fortress. Museums, workshops and cafés line Kristiinankatu as well as *Pokrova* – the oldest Orthodox Baroque church in Finland dating from 1785 *(June–mid Aug Tue–Sun 10am–5pm)*. A 🕐 *nature trail* has been laid out through this district.

THE WOLKOFF FAMILY HOUSE AND MUSEUM

For more that four generations, the Russian merchant family Wolkoff lived in this building from 1826 near the town hall. The house has now been restored room by

room and provides a journey back in time over the past 200 years. The café restaurant serves Russian and Finnish gourmet food in the style of yesteryear *(Expensive)*. *June–Aug Mon–Fri 10am–6pm, Sat/Sun 11am–5pm, Sept–May Sat/Sun 11am–5pm | 5.50 euros | Kauppakatu 26*

LAPPEE CHURCH

This is the last remaining example of a church built on the 'double cruciform' ground plan in 1794, once so typical of Karelia, with a multitude of structural wooden trusses and beams. *June–Aug daily | Valtakatu 35*

ETELÄKARJALAN MUSEO (SOUTH KARELIA MUSEUM)

The museum explains the history and cultural heritage of the province of South Karelia and the importance of Lappeenranta for trade between the East and the West. *June–Aug Mon–Fri 10am–6pm, Sat/Sun 11am–5pm, Sept–May Tue–Sun 11am–5pm | 6.50 euros | Kristiinankatu 15*

SAIMAA LAKE DISTRICT ★

Lake Saimaa is a huge, confusing labyrinth of water. It is not only Finland's largest lake and the centre of Finland's Lake District but, together with numerous rivers and canals, comprises a network of narrow waterways and broad lake estuaries to form Europe's most extensive lakeland area. This body of water was cut off from the Baltic after the last Ice Age as the result of post-glacial rebound. A new sub-species of seal evolved: the Saimaa ringed seal. This rare animal, that lives in fresh water and is endemic to Saimaa, is now threatened with extinction – there are only a few more than 200 left.

The best way to explore Lake Saimaa as a visitor is of course from the water. The choice of boat tours is correspondingly large. The *M/S Camilla (www.karelialines.*

LAPPEENRANTA

fi) and *M/S Faro (www.saimaanristeilyt.fi)* sail regularly. Tours on the *M/S Carelia* and *M/S Kristina Brahe* last for between one and three days and include a trip along the Saimaa Canal to *Vyborg* or *St Petersburg (no visa necessary; sailings May–Sept Tue/Thu, in July also Sat | a copy of your passport must be submitted 3 days before the departure date | 280 euros | www.saimaatravel.fi).*

FOOD & DRINK

CAFÉ MAJURSKA
Like in 'Grandma's parlour': hand-crafted items on the walls, period furniture and home-made cakes and pastries. Tea from the samovar. This café in the Fortress District was once an officers' club. *Daily | Kristiinankatu 1 | Budget*

PRINSESSA ARMAADA
A ship restaurant in the harbour with views of the water, unpretentious fish and meat dishes and snacks. *In summer, daily | Am Passagierhafen | tel. 05 4 513 376 | www.prinsessaarmaada.fi | Moderate*

INSIDER TIP SÄRÄPIRTTI KIPPURASARVI
Located in the little village of Lemi, 20 km (12½ mi) away, this restaurant specialises in the tradtional lamb dish, *särä*, prepared in a birchwood trough. *Rantatie 1 | tel. 05 4 14 64 70 | reservations and opening times under www.sarapirtti.fi | Budget*

WHERE TO STAY

HUHTINIEMI CAMPING
The holiday complex (2 km/1¼ mi from the town) has 20 youth-hostel-style rooms to rent, log cabins for night stays and 2 holiday flats. Lakeside sauna. *Kuusimäenkatu 18 | tel. 05 4 515 55 | www.huhtiniemi.com | Budget*

SCANDIC PATRIA
Pleasant, medium category hotel in a convenient location on the lake and for the harbour. *133 rooms | Kauppakatu 21 | tel. 05 677 511 | www.scandichotels.com/patria | Moderate*

INFORMATION

LAPPEENRANTA TOURIST INFORMATION
Kauppakatu 40 D, Maakuntagalleria | tel. 05 66 77 88 | www.gosaimaa.fi

WHERE TO GO

ASTUVANSALMI ROCK PAINTINGS (127 D3) (ω F12)
The 60 paintings on the rock face on *Lake Yövesi* near *Toijola* (100 km/62 mi away) are more than 5000 years old. First discovered in 1968, the paintings feature northern European shamanic symbols, with pictures of elks, humans, animal tracks and boats. Some of the paintings can only be seen from a boat. Expert guides and boat tours can be arranged on request. *Ancient Tours Ltd. | tel. 045 1 28 17 81 | info@muinaismatkat.fi*

IMATRA (127 E4) (ω G12)
A natural spectacle accompanied by classical music takes place between the end of June and mid August in Imatra (pop. 29,000), 40 km (25 mi) away. The *River Vuoksi*, that, since 1929, has been diverted into a reservoir for hydroelectricity, is the focal point. During the summer months, the flood gates are opened once a day *(6pm)*. The 20-minute spectacle of the Vuoksi racing furiously along its former bed, is set to music by Jean Sibelius. The former state-owned hotel, the luxurious *Rantasipi Imatran Valtionhotelli*, is close by *(137 rooms | Torkkelinkatu 2 | tel. 05 625 20 00 | www.rantasipi.fi | Expensive).*

Fancy sleeping in a museum? That's possible at Verla White Board Mills Museum

MIKKELI (121 D4) (*G12*)

The capital of the East Finland (pop. 49,000), 105 km/65 mi away, is in a beautiful area that is formed by the rivers flowing out of the Saimaa lakeland area. It comes as no surprise really that Mikkeli has the highest concentration of summer houses in Finland. You can get a view of the town, the water and islands from the *viewing tower and café (end May–end Aug daily 10am–7pm | Mikonkatu 23)*. The *Päämajamuseo (Headquarters Museum)* is located nearby. During World War II, the Marshal of Finland, Baron Mannerheim, set up his headquarters in Mikkeli *(May–Aug daily 10am–5pm, otherwise Fri–Sun 10am–5pm | 5 euros | Päämajankuja 1–3)*. The manor house INSIDER TIP *Tertin Kartano* offers elegant accommodation in period style together with award-winning cuisine. The well-tended gardens and lunch in the café make a short visit well worthwhile, too *(5 rooms | Kuopiontie 68 | tel. 015 176 012 | www.tertinkartano.fi | Budget)*. The spa resort *Anttolanhovi*, with its airy beach villas made of Finnish birch and quarried stone with views over Lake Saimaa, is run on a luxury organic principle *(54 rooms, 7 flats, 19 villas | Hovintie 224 | tel. 0207 57 52 00 | www.anttolanhovi.fi | Moderate)*. Information: *Suomen Matkatoimisto Oy | Porrassalmen katu 23 | tel. 010 82 62 46 | www.visitmikkeli.fi*

VERLA WHITE BOARD MILLS
(127 D4) (*F12–13*)

For a century, paper and high-quality board was manufactured behind the red-brick walls in Verla, 80 km (50 mi) away. The factory remained intact even after production was stopped and was converted into a museum. This was done so authentically that this piece of industrial history is now a World Heritage Site. Factory life in the 19th century can be experienced at the turning machinery. Visits are only possible as part of a 1-hour tour *(May–mid Sept Tue–Sun 10am–6pm | 7 euros | Verlantie 295 | www.verla.fi)*. In the evening, you can have the museum grounds to yourself. Cosy holiday homes – also available for overnight stays – have now been made out the former workers' cottages by the adjoining lake. You get the key after paying a deposit of 100 euros at the museum ticket office *(15 cottages, open May–Aug | www.verla.fi/en/cottages | Budget).*

YLÄMÄÄ (127 E4) (*㎝ G13*)

The rare feldspar spectrolite is only found in the south Saimaa area near Ylämää (35 km/22 mi). Meanwhile, half the community has devoted itself to marketing this mineral that shines in all the colours of the rainbow. In the *mineral museum* you can marvel at samples of spectrolite together with other precious stones *(June–Aug daily 10am–5pm | free admission | Jalokivikylä). Kiviseppä (www.kiviseppa.fi)* and *Korukivi (www.korukivi.fi)* sell jewellery and souvenirs. Over the midsummer weekend, a large precious metal fair is held.

SAVONLINNA

(127 E3) (*㎝ G11–12*) **Have fun wherever you happen to be: that's something the people in Savonlinna know a lot about. The town is the setting of the international Opera Festival that attracts people from all around the world. Savonlinna is also known for the Mobile Phone Throwing World Championships.**

The difference between the two events is that, while there are only some 100 participants in the the phone throwing contest, Savolinna (pop. 28,000) is bursting at the seams during the traditional opera festival season. Up to 70,000 visitors descend on the town to listen to *Tosca* or *Tannhäuser* in the picturesque setting of Olavinlinna Castle on the lake. The festival lasts several weeks and whoever wants to visit the town at that time needs to reserve somewhere to stay well in advance. Out of the festival season, Savonlinna is a sleepy, friendly little place.

A medieval Finnish jewel: Olavinlinna Castle

SIGHTSEEING

OLAVINLINNA CASTLE ★
The best-preserved medieval castle in northern Europe and an absolute must, irrespective of the Opera Festival. The fortress, built by the Swedes in 1475, received its present appearance following major restoration work between 1961 and 1975. Olavinlinna houses a History Museum and an Orthodox Museum, congress and festival halls and a beer garden. Guided tours are available, including behind-the-scenes tours during the festival season. *June–mid Aug daily 10am–6pm, otherwise Mon–Fri 10am–4pm, Sat/Sun 11am–4pm | 6 euros | opera tickets (between 80–270 euros): www.operafestival.fi*

FOOD & DRINK

MAJAKKA
Good Finnish fish and meat dishes on the marina. *Daily | Satamakatu 11 | tel. 015 2 06 28 25 | Moderate*

INSIDER TIP MUIKKU BAARI
Grilled whitefish served on wooden platters: let the summer evening on the roof terrace of the *Seurahuone Hotel* begin! *Daily | Kauppatori 4 | tel. 0207 57 13 50 | www.savonlinnanseurahuone.fi | Moderate*

PANIMORAVINTOLA HUVILA
Beer is not only on tap in the summer restaurant of the local brewery with its lovely terrace, but is also used in the kitchen. *Daily | Puistokatu 4 | tel. 015 5 55 05 55 | www.panimoravintolahuvila.fi | Moderate–Expensive*

WHERE TO STAY

LOMAMOKILLA
Stay on a picture-postcard Finnish farm, in a *mökki* on the lake with a sauna or in the guesthouse, either with full board or self-catering. 10 km (6 mi) from the town. *23 rooms, 8 cabins | Mikonkiventie 209 | tel. 015 52 31 17 | www.lomamokkila.fi | Moderate*

PERHEHOTELLI HOSPITZ
A family-run hotel, furnished in the 1930s style. Central, peaceful location with lake views. Lovely orchard, good food and friendly service. *21 rooms | Linnankatu 20 | tel. 015 515 6 61 | www.hospitz.com | Moderate*

INFORMATION

SAVONLINNA MATKAILU OY TOURIST INFORMATION
Puistokatu 1 | tel. 015 51 75 10 | www.savonlinnatravel.com

WHERE TO GO

KERIMÄKI (127 E3) (𝄞 G11)
3000 people can easily fit inside the largest wooden church in the world (21 km/13 mi away), allegedly built this size by accident. The builder misread the dimensions which were in feet, thinking they were in metres. *June–Aug daily 10am–6pm, July until 7pm | Halvantie*

KUOPIO (127 D1) (𝄞 F10)
Kuopio (pop. 92,000), 150 km/93 mi away, lies surrounded by forests and lakes on a headland projecting into Lake Kallavesi. One of Finland's most attractive boat tours starts (or end) here. A trip with the old ● *M/S Pujo* takes you along canals, through locks and beautiful lakeland country *(end June–mid Aug | Mon/Wed/Fri from Savonlinna, Tue/Thu/Sat from Kuopio, 9am | from 135 euros per person, with overnight accommodation 180 euros | www.mspuijo.fi)*. There are more than 20 other boat trips into the surrounding area that also leave from the harbour.

Kuopio itself is a modern commercial hub with sprawling residential areas. INSIDER TIP ► *Kuopion Korttelimuseo (Old Kuopio Open-Air Museum)* includes a block of houses from the original wooden town. Several buildings are from the katu | tel. 017 19 51 11 | www.scandichotels. com/kuopio | *Moderate*) provides comfortable accommodation with a view of the lake. Information: *Kuopio-Info | Haapaniemenkatu 17 | tel. 017 18 25 84 | www. kuopioinfo.fi*

Birches are synonymous with the Finnish countryside. This one is in Punkaharju

18th century *(mid May–end Aug Tue–Sun 10am–5pm, otherwise 10am–3pm | 4 euros | Kirkkokatu 22 | www.kortteli museo.fi)*. The market square – one of the largest in the country – forms the centre of the town and has a lovely Art Nouveau market building *(Mon–Fri 8am–5pm, Sat 8am–3pm)*. This is where you can by the speciality *kalakukko*, baked fish or meat in a delicious rye crust. In the evening, a visit to one of the best places to dine in the country – the rustically decorated gourmet restaurant *Musta Lammas* – can be recommended *(Mon–Sat | Satamakatu 4 | tel. 017 581 04 58 | Expensive)*. *Café Kaneli* with its wingbacked chairs and open fireplace is perfect for a relaxed cup of coffee *(daily | Kauppakatu 22)*. The Kuopio Scandic Hotel *(138 rooms | Satama-

LINNANSAARI NATIONAL PARK
(127 E2–3) (ᗰ G11)

40ki (25 mi) north of Savonlinna is one of the three, large, inland lake nature reserves in Finland. The national park's 130 islands lie in Lake Haukivesi and are used by the acutely endangered Saimaa seal as a nursery. The small population of this species on the verge of extinction lives in the norther part of the lake. If you are lucky, you may be able to watch them – as well as the osprey or the endangered white-backed woodpecker – when you're on a hike. The park can only be reached by boat. A regular boat service operates during the high season (June–Aug) from Rantasaari and Oravi. Guided tours, campsite and boat hire: *Oskari visitors' centre | Ohitustie 7, Rantasalmi*

PUNKAHARJU ⭐ (127 E3) (*𝄞 G11*)

The area around the narrow, 7 km-long (4½ mi) Punkaharju ridge near the village of the same name (pop. 3700), is a conservation area of national importance and is unreservedly worth seeing. In addition, the exhibitions in the subterranean caves in the *Retretti Museum* are a cultural highlight (*June–Aug daily 10am–6pm | 16 euros | Tuunaan-saarentie 3 | www.retretti.fi*). *Luosto Forestry Museum* illustrates the importance of forestry for Finland (*June–Aug daily 10am–7pm, otherwise Tue–Sun until 5pm | 10 euros | Lustontie 1 | www.lusto.fi*). Accommodation is available in many of the lovely old wooden buildings and manorial farmhouses in the area. Information: *Punkaharju tourist information office | Kauppatie 20 | tel. 015 5 27 54 00 | www.punkaharju.fi*

TAMPERE

(126 B3) (*𝄞 D12*) **'The green heart of Finland' is how the lake district between Vanajavesi and Näsijärvi is sometimes also called, and Tampere (pop. 220,000) is its economic and cultural centre.**

In the 19th century, the town was a pioneer in Finland's industrialisation. It all started in 1783 with the first paper factory, followed in 1820 by the first cotton mill and, in 1882, the first manufacturing plant for lightbulbs. The factory buildings are now occupied by theatres, restaurants and museums which profit from the unique atmosphere behind the brick façades of these industrial monuments.

SIGHTSEEING

AMURIN TYÖLÄISMUSEOKORTELLI (WORKING DISTRICT MUSEUM)

Nowhere in Finland was the workers' movement as strong as in Tampere in the 19th century. 30 buildings with their original furnishings trace the lives of the working class from 1880 until the 1970s. *Mid May–mid Sept Tue–Sun 10am–6pm | affiliated café daily 10am–6pm, in winter 10am–5pm | 6 euros | Satakunnankatu 49*

TUOMIOKIRKKO (CATHEDRAL)

The building from 1907 designed by Lars Sonck in the National Romantic style and built of artistically arranged dressed granite blocks, is outstanding. Its pointed red towers are a landmark and the coloured stained glass windows and interior are masterpieces of Finnish Symbolism. *May–Aug daily 10am–5pm, Sept–April daily 11am–3pm | Tuomiokirkonkatu 3*

FINLAYSON FACTORY

There are any number of historical industrial sites in Tampere. One of the most impressive is the former factory of the Finlayson textile manufacturer and its huge production halls. It is fitting that the workers' museum, among other amenities, is housed on this site today (*Wed 5pm–6.30pm, Sun noon–3pm | free entrance*). One of the company's owners had the nearby church erected solely for his workers. The site also includes the factory manager's villa (*tours Mon 4.30–6pm*). The opulence of this upper classes can also be found in the adjoining restaurant (*Tue–Sat | tel. 0400 21 95 30 | www.finlaysoninpalatsi.com | Moderate*). *Satakunnankatu*

INSIDER TIP ▶ KALEVALA CHURCH AND METSO TOWN LIBRARY

The church to the east of the centre is a place of pilgrimage for lovers of modern architecture. When the radically minimalistic building, designed by the husband and wife team of architects, Reima und Raili Pietilä, was inaugurated in 1966, it unleashed a hefty controversy. The ground plan of the light-infused concrete building is in the shape of the Christian symbol of a fish. The interior is lit by 18 narrow windows and the sole contrasting colour comes from the pine pews *(daily 11am–3pm | Liisanpuisto 1, Teiskontie)*. Those who want to investigate the work of the Pietiläs in more detail, should pay ● a visit to Metso Town Library in the district of Hervanta. The building of brick, copper and glass (1985) is shaped like a capercaillie *(metso)*, and an eye-opener amid the sobre suburban architectural surroundings *(Mon–Fri 10am–8pm, Sat 10am–4pm | Pirkankatu 2)*.

KESKUSTORI MARKET SQUARE

This central square is more or less Tampere's 'front room'. The times when markets were held every day may well be past, but the old market building from 1901 is a proud Art Nouveau testimony to them *(Mon–Fri 8am–6pm, Sat 8am–3pm | Hämeenkatu 19)*. The oldest building on the square is a wooden church from 1824; the town hall nearby is from 1890. A manifesto against Russian suppression was read out from the balcony during the General Strike of 1905.

VAPRIKKI MUSEUM CENTRE

Everything here revolves around the history of the town. Several top-quality exhibitions are united under one roof: the Museum of Technology, the Natural History Museum, the Finnish Shoe Museum, the Ice Hockey Museum, etc. You can certainly spend the whole day here. *Tue–Sun 10am–6pm | 8 euros | Alaverstaanraitti 5 | www.tampere.fi/vaprikki*

FOOD & DRINK

THE GRILL

This 'in' eatery temps guests with delicious char-grilled food in modern surroundings hung with works of art by Teemu Saukkonen. Lovely summer terrace between brick façades. *Daily | Frenckellin Aukio | tel. 03 2 60 33 55 | Moderate–Expensive*

INSIDER TIP HELLA & HUONE

A gourmet restaurant which uses classic ingredients such as wild duck, pickerel or pumpkin to create surprising dishes. The set-menus of several courses have an excellent reputation nationally *(Closed Sun/Mon | Salhojankatu 48 | tel. 010 3 22 38 98 | www.hellajahuone.fi | Expensive)*. Deli shop with salads and sandwiches: *Rautatienkatu 27.*

VOHVELIKAHVILA

Nostalgic waffle bakery with a lot of flair. Sweet and savoury temptations accompanied by changing art exhibitions. *Daily | Ojakatu 2 | Budget*

Shopping in Art Nouveau surroundings: the market building in Tampere

INSIDER TIP **4 VUODENAIKAA**

The 'Four Seasons' is a popular French bistro in the market building serving lunches. The ingredients come straight from the neighbouring stands. *Closed Sun | Hämeenkatu 19 | tel. 03 212 47 12 | Budget–Moderate*

SHOPPING

Tampere was the first place in Finland to be named a 🕐 fair trade town – with such products available throughout the town. In the listed market building you will find regional specialities and fresh local produce *(Mon–Fri 8am–6pm, Sat 8am–3pm | Hämeenkatu 19)*.

SPORTS & ACTIVITIES

SEITSEMINEN AND HELVENTINJÄRVI NATIONAL PARKS

Lake Näsijärvi is an extensive body of water north of Tampere. This is where these two smaller national parks are located. *Seitseminen* (16 mi²) combines biotopes of primeval forests, wetlands and ponds, and has a well-signposted circular route (8 km/5 mi) through it. *Helventinjärvi* (11½ mi²) gives a clue about its main attraction in its name: *Helventinkolu* means 'Hell's crevasse'. This is actually a deep gorge with a lake for swimming in at the bottom. A 40 km-long (25 mi) network of paths criss-crosses the park. Information: *www.outdoors.fi*

PYYNIKKI AND PISPALA

Where a glacier ended in the Ice Age is not the highest terminal moraine in Europe. To the south west of the centre on the north bank of Lake Pyhäjärvi, Pyynikki towers 85 m (279 ft) above surface of the lake. The moraine is richly forested and steep. At the top there is a ☀ viewing tower with a café *(daily 9am–8pm)* as well as a park, to the west is the old working-class district of Pispala with its nostalgic wooden

TAMPERE

houses. The twisting lanes in Pispala lead both to the ridge as to Finland's oldest, public wood sauna, which has been in operation since 1906 *(Rajaportin Sauna | Mon/Wed 6pm–10pm, Fri 3pm–9pm, Sat 2pm–10pm | 4–6 euros | Pispalan valtatie 9 | www.pispala.fi/rajaportinsauna).*

SÄRKÄNNIEMI

Tampere's 'Tivoli' is located on Lake Näsijärvi. In summer; the big dippers, merry-go-rounds and water slides in Särkänniemi leisure park open at noon; the delfinarium, aquarium and planetarium are open all the year round. The ☼ revolving restau-

noon–7pm, otherwise Tue–Sun 11am–6pm | 7 euros | Laiturikatu 13). Information: *www.sarkanniemi.fi*

VIIKANSAARI

This little, wooded island in Lake Pyhäjärvi is Tampere's most popular local recreational area. Beaches and barbecue areas, footpaths and children's playgrounds, saunas and boats for hire: everything is here. In summer, the weekend gets off to a good start on the dance floor with humppa music and waltzes. *Boat connections June–Aug Tue–Sun from 10am every hour from Laukantori jetty | www.hopealinja.fi*

A lively fun day out at Särkänniemi leisure park

rant at the top of the tower is also open all year. From here you have the best view of the lake district in which Tampere is situated *(in summer daily 11am–11pm | Expensive).* The excellent Sara Hildén art museum is also in the park. It houses works by modern masters such as Klee, Bacon and Picasso and temporary exhibitions of works by unknown artists *(summer daily*

WHERE TO STAY

HOSTEL SOFIA

Centrally located near the cathedral and station. This recently renovated youth hostel provides cheap and friendly accommodation. *28 rooms | Tuomiokirkonkatu 12 A | tel. 03 2 54 40 20 | www.hostelsofia. fi | Budget*

HOTEL MANGO

There is no reception; booking is done on the Internet. The hotel service is good, the rooms cosy. *26 rooms | Hatanpään Puistokuja 36 | tel. 03 2 14 28 34 | www.mango hotel.fi | Budget*

HOTEL VICTORIA

Well-looked-after hotel where Finnish artists and locals also stay. Generous breakfast. *71 rooms | Itsenäisyydenkatu 1 | tel. 03 2 42 51 11 | www.hotellivictoria.fi | Moderate*

INFORMATION

TAMPERE TOURIST INFORMATION

Rautatienkatu 25 A (Hauptbahnhof) | tel. 03 56 56 68 00 | www.gotampere.fi

WHERE TO GO

INSIDER TIP ▶ FRANTSILA HERB FARM ☺
(127 B3) (*ℳ D12*)

The oldest herb farm in Finland (38 km/ 23½ mi) has a café and garden, a shop and a summer terrace on the banks of the River *Hämeenkyrö (closed Sun | Yrjö-Koskisentie 1 | www.frantsilankehakukka. fi)*. In the ● spa near the fields of herbs, let yourself be spoilt with a shiatsu and herbal sauna. The traditional Finnish 'limb alignment' – kalevalainen jäsenkorjaus – is also available *(Kyrös-pohjantie 320 | appointments: tel. 040 5 91 87 42 | www.frantsilanhyvanolonkeskus.fi)*

HÄMEENLINNA
(126 B4) (*ℳ E13*)

The 'Castle of Häme' gave the town (pop. 67,000) its name. Located 80 km (50 mi) away, it is where Jean Sibelius' birthplace can be seen *(May–Aug daily 10am–4pm, otherwise Tue–Sun noon–4pm | 4 euros | Hallituskatu 11 | www.sibelius.fi)*. Aulanko leisure centre on the edge of a park is pleasant for a night's stay and has a spa, swimming pool and golf course *(www. aulanko.fi)*. The white Silver Line ships operate between Hämeenlinna and Tampere and also call in at Aulanko on their way.

IITTALA
(126 B4) (*ℳ E13*)

In the little village of Iittala (55 km/34 mi), the success story of Finnish glass design began in 1881. This is where the famous Aalto vases, among other items, are produced. You can watch the glass-blowers working in the Iittala factory *(guided tours mid May–end Aug by reserving in advance: tel. 0204 39 62 30 | Könnölänmäentie)*. There is also a glass museum adjoining. *(May–Aug daily 10am–6pm, Sept–April Sat/Sun 10am–5pm)*. Seconds, products with slight irregularities, can be purchased in the factory outlet at reduced prices.

THE SILVER LINE AND THE POET'S ROUTE

If you have time, go on a mini cruise from Tampere. There are two routes to choose from: the white ships of the *Silver Line* depart from Laukantori quay in the morning and go as far as Hämeenlinna. The return trip by bus can be booked at the same time. Reservations are recommended *(68 euros incl. return bus journey | www.hopealinja.fi)*.

The *Poet's Route (runoilijan tie)* sets off from Mustalahti quay for the Näsijärvi area. During the eight-hour trip, the steamer chugs to Virrat through countryside whose virtues have been praised in many a song. A stop in the INSIDER TIP ▶ remotely situated country studio of the famous 19th-century Finnish Romantic painter, *Akseli Gallen-Kallela*, who fled here to escape city life, is also included on the tour. *53 euros Tampere–Virrat, return journey for half the price | www.runoilijantie.fi*

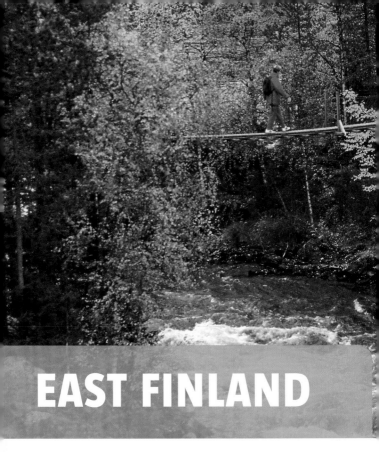

EAST FINLAND

To the north of the Finnish lake district, the patchwork of bays, islands, forests and lakes carries on. Unadulterated nature awaits visitors between Kainuu and North Karelia.

It is a region in which the bear is just as much at home as the elk, lynx and wolf. Economically speaking, the area has a poor infrastructure, but ecologically it is a treasure trove. The extensive forests, moors and lakes are the habitat of many rare animals and plants. Man has largely left the wilderness alone in the east. In this stretch of land there are only a few scattered settlements along the Russian border. Villages and farms are far apart

and, in the northeastern-most corner of the EU the Orthodox faith has become mixed together with Finnish and Russian traditions. There is always a place for stories to be told in the ever-prevalent silence. For this reason, the east is also the cradle of mythology. This is where the national epic *Kalevala* has its roots.

KAINUU

Some people simply pass through the endless forests around Kainuu on their way north. But they are missing out on a unique experience.

Photo: Oulanka National Park

A visit to the wolves and lynxes: experience the power of untamed nature in the forests of Kainuu and North Karelia

The Kainuu region lies between the Gulf of Bothnia, Lapland, Karelia and the lake district. In the 19th century, the forests and the poor charcoal-burners of Kainuu supplied the tar needed for the fleets of ships in Europe. The 'black gold' was put in vessels and transported by boat to Oulu. Today, the industry has disappeared and the forests of Kainuu are even too lonely for the Finns who prefer to holiday in the south. This region has therefore become a paradise for die-hard wilderness fanatics, for nature photographers and for those looking for somewhere remote.

KAJAANI (129 E4) *(🗺 F9)*
This, the largest town in Kainuu (pop. 38,000), was founded in 1651. It lies on

KAINUU

Elias Church in Ilomantsi is at
the very heart of North Karelia

the River Kajaani between the lakes
Oulujärvi and Nuasjärvi. The tar channel
from 1846 in *Karoliinenpark* is a reminder
of the days of tar transport, the *castle ruins*
on an island in the river, of the conflicts
with Russia. *Kajaani church* (1896), with its
ornate woodwork, is one of the most attractive Gothic Revival buildings *(June–Aug
daily 10am–8pm | Kirkkokatu 19)*. *Kahvila
Pekka Heikkinen* café, on the other hand,
is plain but its cakes and rye bread are
baked in a traditional wood oven. A spe-
ciality are the tar chocolates. *(Daily | Väli-
katu 7)*. *Sirius* in Villa Koskikara is well
known for its regional food *(closed Sat/
Sun | Brahenkatu 5 | tel. 08 6 12 20 87 |
Budget)*. You can stay in *Scandic Kajanus*
which has large rooms and a pool *(191
rooms | Koskikatu 3 | tel. 08 6 16 41 | www.
scandichotels.fi/kajanus | Moderate)* or in
the elegant Manor *Hotel Karolineburg* with
a view of the river *(20 rooms | Karoliinantie
4 | tel. 08 6 13 12 91 | www.karolineburg.
com | Budget–Moderate)*.

Information: *Kajaani Info Kauppakatu 21 |
tel. 08 61 55 25 55 | www.visitkajaani.fi*

KUHMO (129 F5) (*ळ G9*)

This small town (pop. 10,000) is well
known for its chamber music festival and
Kalevala Adventure Park, where the spirit
of the national epic poem, among other
works, is brought to life and where you
can enjoy delicacies cooked on birchwood
boards in the village with its collection of
little huts *(www.kalevalaspirit.fi)*. An ex-
planation of Kalevala can be foiund in
*Juminkeko information centre (Sun–Thu
noon–6pm, July daily | Kontionkatu 25 |
www.juminkeko.fi)*. 3 km (2 mi) from the
centre you can find out all about wild animals, the forest and forestry in the *Petola
Nature Centre*. The fortress-like *Hotel Kale-
vala (47 rooms | Väinämöinen 9 | tel. 08 65
51 00 | www.hotellikalevala.fi | Moderate)*
has comfortable rooms with lake views.
Large predators feel particularly at home
in the undisturbed border area near Kuhmo.
If you want to experience the bear, wolf
and lynx in their natural environment first
hand and capture everything on film, your
best chance for spectacular pictures is to
take part on a INSIDER TIP bear-watching
tour. The nature photographer Lassi Rau-
tianinen has specialised in the bear, but
also wolves, wolverines and capercaillies
walk in front of his lens. Accommodation
on the photo safari is in cabins in the forest
*(200–300 euros per person | www.arctic
media.fi.)*. A wider range can be found,
for example, under *www.taigaspirit.com*,
www.erapiira.fi or *www.wildbrownbear.fi*.
If you leave Kuhmo and head north, you
will have INSIDER TIP a strange encounter
in the area around Suomussalmi: as if by
magic, suddenly a mass of people, almost
one thousand in all, appear at the side of
the road. The individual figures have straw
for hair and are battered by the wind, the
sun shines on their turf faces, their clothes

hang on wooden bodies. Depending on the time of day, the 'silent people' *(Hiljainen kansa)* can seem either grumpy, happy or pensive. And each time you have the feeling that they are alive.

The figures are an installation by the artist Reijo Kela. And what does it mean? That's a question of interpretation. One clue is that when it comes to the figures being given their annual change of clothes, the 1000 wooden figures become 1000 wooden crosses. Suomussalmi, the home of the 'silent people', is in an area where there were bitter fights during World War II. *Field café: mid June–mid Aug 9am–9pm*

NORTH KARELIA

Historic Karelia between the Baltic and the White Sea was, for many centuries, a bone of contention between Russians, Swedes and Finns. Since World War II only North and South Karelia, the area around Lappeenranta, belong to Finland.

The Karelians, like the Sami, are one of the indigenous people of northern Europe. Their mythical places and stories have become part of the national epic *Kalevala* which, to this day, is a work of the utmost significance for the Finnish people.

SIGHTSEEING

ILOMANTSI (127 F2) (*∅ H10*)

In the eastern-most community (pop. 5900) is the ● runic singers' village *Parppeinvaara*, an open-air museum for Karelian culture and tradition *(June–Aug 10am–4pm, July until 6pm | 5 euros | Parppeintie 4 | www.parppeinvaara.fi)*. Folk tunes can be heard performed on the *kantele*, the Finnish zither, familiar from *Kalevala*. The *Parppeinpirtti restaurant*

serves buffet lunches with Karelian specialites and à la carte meals *(June/Aug daily, otherwise closed Sat/Sun | tel. 013 88 14 21 | Moderate)*. *Elias church*, with ist six onion towers, is the largest Orthodox church made of wood *(mid June–mid Aug daily 11.30am–5pm | Kirkkotie)*. Fine spirits can be combined with a lovely view in ⋋ the tower restaurant in the Hermanni berry winery *(June–mid Aug daily 10am–10pm | Kappalaisentie | tel. 0207 78 92 33 | www.hermanninviinitila.fi | Budget–Moderate)*. If you stay at the Karelian Anssila Maatila farm you can bed down with the dogs, chickens and cats *(32 beds | Anssilantie 7 | tel. 040 5 43 15 26 | www.ilomantsi.com/anssila | Budget)*. Information: *Karelia Expert | Kalevalantie 13 | tel. 0400 24 00 72 | ilomantsi@kareliaexpert.fi*

JOENSUU (127 F2) (*∅ G11*)

The largest town in North Karelia (pop. 73,000) is idyllically located at the estuary of the River Pielinen on Lake Pyhäselkä. It is an industrial centre and a university town with a theatre, art museum and ambitious

MARCO POLO HIGHLIGHTS

⭐ **Koli National Park**
Fantastic view from the Ukkokoli rocky outcrop
→ p. 84

⭐ **Uusi Valamo**
The monastery is the centre of the Finnish Orthodox Church in beautiful surrounds
→ p. 85

⭐ **Oulanka National Park**
Bears, wolves and eagles: welcome to this famous untamed natural paradise
→ p. 86

The view from Ukkokoli is breathtaking

building projects, Apart from a few remaining buildings, the old wooden town has had to make way for large blocks of flats and offices. The *North Karelia Museum (Pohjois-Karjalan Museo)* traces the history and culture of Karelia in exhibitions, sound recording of runic singing, local costume and photos *(Mon–Fri 10am–5pm, Sat/Sun 10am–3pm | Koskikatu 5 | 5 euros)*.

On the eastern bank on the edge of the town, the new district of Pentilä has been built on the site of a former sawmill. The evening sun can be enjoyed the longest, the best view of the river is to be found and good Italian/Finnish food in the restaurant *La Passione* (with delicatessen shop): *Tue–Sat | Pentillänranta, Vallilanauko 2 | tel. 010 4 39 44 00 | Moderate*. If you prefer to stay in the centre: in *Teatteriravintola*, an imposing town house from 1914 with a conservatory, good Karelian and international meals are served *(closed Sat/ Sun | Rantakatu 20 | tel. 013 2 56 69 00 | Moderate)*. The *summer café Jokiasema* is on the estuary with a lovely view of the lake *(May–Sept daily | Hasanniementie 3 | Budget)*. Kesähotelli Elli has simple, bright rooms with a shower, WC and breakfast for rent *(80 rooms | June–Aug | Länsikatu 18 | tel. 010 4 21 56 00 | www.summerhotelelli. fi | Budget)*. The new ☺ *Greenstar Hotel* in a low-energy building has an automatic check-in, the rooms are bright and furnished in the Scandinavian style, breakfast is available to order. *(82 rooms | Torikatu 16 | tel. 010 4 23 93 90 | www.greenstar.fi | Budget)*. Information: *Carelicum & Karelia Expert | Koskikatu 5 | tel. 0400 23 95 49 | www.kareliaexpert.fi*

KOLI NATIONAL PARK
⭐ (129 F6) (*ω G10*)

The wooded range of hills around the rocky outcrop *Ukkokoli* (347 m/1138 ft), with a view across the vast expanse of Lake Pielinen to Russia, is now one of Finland's protected national parks. The view from the rooms in the Hotel Koli is correspondingly impressive *(75 rooms, 27 cabins | Ylä-Kolintie 39 | tel. 020 123 46 62 | Moderate–*

Expensive). A visitor centre provides tourists with information about the park and it flora and fauna. Cross-country tracks are prepared and sledge safaris organised in winter; an ice road even leads across the frozen lake – in summer there is a ferry. Information: *Koli-Info | Ylä-Kolintie 2, Koli | tel. 045 138 74 29 | www.koli.fi*

JUUKA (129 F6) *(📗 G10)*

In Juuka soapstone is quarried and made into wood-burners. Geological exhibitions, souvenirs and a restaurant are located right on the E6 *(mid June–Ende Aug Sun–Fri 9am–6pm, Sat 9am–4pm, May/Sept/Oct until 5pm | Kuhnustantie 10 | www.kivikyla.fi)*.

LIEKSA (129 F6) *(📗 G10)*

This little town (pop. 15,000) would not be worth visiting as such, if it were not so spread out: you can enjoy the natural surroundings anywhere in Lieksa. The most important sites are the *Pielinen open-air museum*, that is on a peninsula in the river. 70 buildings from three centuries are on display here and show how the Karelians once lived – from the rafters to the big land owners *(mid May–mid Sept daily 10am–6pm | 5 euros | Pappilantie 2)*.

25 km (15½ mi) east of the centre, the Lieksanjoki changes into a whitewater river at the *Ruunaa rapids*. The surrounding area is popular among canoeists, anglers and hikers. Information, boats and accommodation: *Ruuna Visitor Centre (Ruunaantie 129, Pankakoski | tel. 0205 64 57 57 | www.ruunaa.fi)*.

30 km (19 mi) further south in the village of Paateri is the INSIDER TIP home and studio of the renowened Finnish sculptress Eva Ryynänen (1915–2001). The petite artist made sculptures from huge tree trunks which she imported from Russia. Animals, scenes and figures from Finnish mythology as well as her largest work – a wooden church with an altar made of roots – can all be marvelled at here *(May–Sept daily 10am–6pm | 4 euros | Paateri 21, Vuonisjärvi bei Lieksa)*.

UUSI VALAMO ⭐ (121 E2) *(📗 G11)*

The monastery is a branch of the Orthodox monastery, Valamo, in Russia. Some 200 monks fled the original monastery island in the Winter War of 1940 and founded 'New Valamo' in Heinävesi. And so a piece of Russian culture and religious art continues to flourish through the monks in what is now the only monastery for men of the Finnish Orthodox Church. Visitors can visit the complex with its golden onion towers, join in services of worship and, in July, are invited to join the monks for a Russian tea. Basic accommodation is also available *(daily 7am–9pm | Moderate)*. The Orthodox nuns in *Lintula Convent* nearby are more reclusive but this outpost of the Eastern Orthodox Church can also be visited. There are souvenirs, a café and the possibility for religious discussion. *Valamo Monastery: daily | Valamontie 42 | tel. 017 57 0111 | www.valamo.fi; Lintula Convent: June–Aug daily | Honkasalontie 3, Palokki*

LOW BUDGET

▶ A flexible shared taxi *(Kimpataxi)* costing 19 euros operates three times a day between Joensuu, Koli, Juuka and Lieksa. *Reservation 24 hours in advance necessary | tel. 0100 99 86 (*) | information: tel. 040 7 71 66 52*

▶ The Pulla Puoti bakery in Joensuu has the freshest, best and cheapest pastries and pancakes around. *Merimiehenkatu 26*

THE NORTH EAST

In the vast expanse of the North East, traces of human life disappear. Here it is possible to enjoy the natural environment in its unadulterated form and this is where one of the best known hiking trails, the 'Bear's Ring' *(Karhunkierros)* can be found.
The North East *(koillismaa)* borders on Lapland. The climate and landscape are very Nordic in character; the nights in summer unbelievably bright, with extensive snowfall in the bitterly cold months from October. The best time to visit is when the plagues of mosquitoes have died off from mid August onwards and the leaves have started to get their autumn colours – their *ruska*.

SIGHTSEEING

KUUSAMO (129 E2) *(ᗅ G7)*

Kuusamo (pop. 17,000) is the largest town in the North East. There are three national parks in the vicinity. The airport is a logistic hub for visitors and local industry. The INSIDER TIP Centre for Nature Photography, with marvellous pictures taken by the famous Finnish photographer Hannu Hautala, is worth a visit *(end June–end Sept Mon–Fri 9am–5pm, Sat 10am–2pm, Sun noon–4pm | 4 euros | Torangintaival 2, Karhuntassu Information Centre)*. The *game restaurant Riipisen* serves fish as well as game in a wooden cabin at the Kelo lift in Ruka *(daily | Rukatunturintie 6 | tel. 08 8 68 12 19 | Moderate–Expensive)*. A meal in the *Studio Restaurant Tundra* prepared by the head chef Jarmo Pitkänen is a feast for all the senses *(reservations 1 day in advance, min. 2 people | Vuotungintie 152 | tel. 040 7 73 80 00 | Expensive)*. *Isokenkaisten Klubi* is a friendly log cabin hotel near Särkiluoma on the Russian border

(17 rooms, 3 cabins | Heikinjärventie 3 | tel. 0400 97 22 60 | www.ikk.fi | Moderate).

INSIDER TIP JULMA ÖLKKY
(129 E2) *(ᗅ G7)*

The cliffs that frame Julma Ölkky, a lake in a ravine, are a sheer 50m drop. This 3 km-long (2 mi) stretch of water is a mere 20 m wide at the narrowest point and reaches a depth of 40m. Rainbows are formed by light falling on the streams flowing into it on the precipitous eastern side. Guided boat tours over the lake are available in summer. *Mid June–mid Aug daily 10am–7pm, until end of Aug 10am–4pm | 12 euros | www.julmaolkky.fi*

OULANKA NATIONAL PARK ★ ●
(129 E–F1) *(ᗅ G6)*

The glacial Oulanjoki river landscape with its waterfalls, gorges, lichen-covered primeval forest and many rare animals and plants is a famous untamed paradise. The national park is part of the ☺ Pan Parks Foundation *(www.panparks.org)*, that aims to protect the last, great areas

of wilderness in Europe while promoting sustainable tourism. Wolves, bears and eagles live in the park, and in the northern peatlands, the rare cloudberry can be found.

The park is known to passionate hikers due to the 'Bear's Ring', one of the most famous trails. The 80 km-long (50 mi) route (which is not a circular tour!) leads through undisturbed forests past rapids, waterfalls and canyons. Depending on how fit you are, the time you have and the weather, you can either complete the whole tour (approx. 5 days), divide it into sections or take the short, 12 km-long (7½ mi) 'little Bear's Ring' (pieni karhunkierros). Those on the main tour can sleep in shelters and clear signposting along the way means that it is virtually impossible to lose your way. A good place to start is the Oulanka visitors's centre, the village of Juuma or Ristikallio in the north.

The best time for the 'Bear's Ring' is during the *ruska* in autumn, when the leaves of the aspen, rowan and birch turn into brilliant shades of colour.

Even if you prefer to take things more gently, you should still make for this park – the informative nature centre alone is well-worth a visit. Apart from a kiosk, café and cabins for rent there is a short, easy path (1 km) that leads to the Kiutaköngäs rapids that should not be missed. *Oulanka Nature Centre | Liikasenvaarantie 32, Kuusamo | tel. 0205 64 68 50 | www.outdoors.fi*

RUKA
(129 E2) (*∅ G7*)

Ruka is the sport centre of this area and one of the major winter sports arenas. You have a choice of 28 pistes and a world-cup mogul slope, tracks and snoeshoe trails, as well as many holiday houses, restaurants and other activities. Mount Rukantunturi towers 500 m over Ruka and is the starting point for a 1000 m-long summer toboggan run down into the valley. In summer many hikers set off from here on various trails, including the 'Bear's Ring'. *Ruka Info | Rukankyläntie 8 | tel. 08 8 60 02 00 | www.ruka.fi*

Longing for the winter: the beautiful countryside around Ruka in the morning light

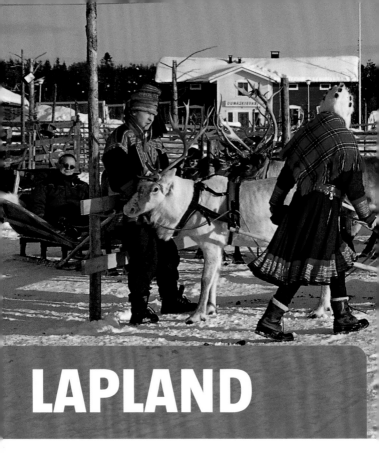

LAPLAND

The wild natural beauty of the far north: this is Lapland. Most of this region lies north of the Arctic Circle and, with just 184,000 inhabitants, is extremely sparsely populated.

For eight months of the year, ice and snow dictate life in Lapland. In the dark winter nights, the northern lights appear in the sky – glowing symphonies of colour, around which many a myth has been spun. The native inhabitants of the region, the Sami, called these lights *revontuli*, meaning 'fox fire'. One of their sagas tells of a fox that painted the colours in the night sky with its tail. From February onwards, the days start to get longer. A snowy landscape glistening in the sun can be explored on a snowmobile, a reindeer or dog sled, or on skis. The short summer starts in July and lasts until the beginning of September with its fiery autumn foliage – *ruska*. Wilderness fans, canoeists, fishermen and gold seekers brave clouds of mosquitoes to be able to experience Europe's last truly wild region.

INARI

(131 D3) (*⃞ F3*) Lake Inari is the third largest lake in Finland – a place of special importance to the Sami that has given its name to the surrounding community.

Photo: Reindeer farm in Lapland

In the land of the midnight sun: Lapland's magic is to be found in its wide open spaces and untouched scenery

The lake covers 1040 km² and is peppered with some 3000 islands. The vegetation around its shore – pine, spruce and birch trees – only reach dwarf proportions. The climate is marked by freezing cold temperatures well into spring. The area is correspondingly thinly populated. Inari has a population of only 7000 – that statistically means just 1.2 people per mi². 30 percent of the inhabitants of Inari are Sami.

They live from fishing, reindeer farming and tourism, and try to hang onto their cultural inheritance in a balancing act between the traditional and modern world.

SIGHTSEEING

SIIDA SÁMI MUSEUM ★
The museum provides an overview of the history, way of living and culture of the

The Lemmenjoki National Park can also be explored by boat

Sami people. Buildings, animals traps and everyday objects can be seen in the open-air museum. *June–Sept daily 9am–8pm, Oct–May Tue–Sun 10am–5pm | Inarintie 46 | 8 euros | www.siida.fi.* The *North Lapland Nature Centre* is housed in the same building.

FOOD & DRINK

INSIDER TIP NUTUKAS

Cosy café and lunch-time restaurant in a former bank. *Daily | Ivalontie 2, Ivalo | tel. 040 162 25 99 | Budget*

PETRONELLA

This restaurant serves excellent 'gold-digger' specialities and good wines. *Daily | Honkapolku 5, Saariselkä | tel. 016 66 89 30 | Moderate–Expensive*

WHERE TO STAY

HOTEL INARIN KULTAHOVI

Pleasant, family-run hotel. 29 rooms in the main building; the 16 rooms in the building on the bank all have a view of the river. Good restaurant with regional fare. *Saari-koskentie 2, Inari | tel. 016 5 11 71 00 | www.hotelkultahovi.fi | Moderate–Expensive*

INSIDER TIP VILLA LANCA B & B

Imaginatively furnished wooden villa run by a Finnish/Sami couple. Breakfast in the wine bar and restaurant. *2 rooms, 3 flats | Kittilän Ratsutie 2, Inari | tel. 040 7 48 09 84 | www.villalanca.com | Moderate*

INFORMATION

TOURIST INFORMATION OFFICE

Inari: *Siida Museum | Inarintie 46;* Ivalo: *Ivalontie 10 | tel. 040 168 96 68;* Saariselkä/Kiehinen: *Kelotie 1 | tel. 040 168 78 38*

WHERE TO GO

INSIDER TIP KARHUNPESÄKIVI (BEAR'S DEN STONE) (131 D3) (ØØ F3)

This cave inside a huge boulder is a natural wonder located in an untouched forest area along with other rocks and boulders 20 km (12½ mi) south of Inari. It can be easily reached along a boardwalk from the café on the E75 between Inari and Ivalo.

BOAT TRIPS ON THE LEMMENJOKI ★ (131 D3) (ØØ E4)

At the time of the gold rush, the Sami transported gold diggers and their supplies up the River Lemmenjoki in narrow long boats to the prospecting grounds. Since 1956, the area has been part of *Lemmenjoki National Park* – at 1,100 mi², the most extensive and untamed area of protected countryside in Finland. Although there are still some prospectors here today, most of the people the Sami take along the untouched river valley to *Ravadasköngäs Waterfall* or to the old gold diggers' huts in *Hamina* are hikers and day tourists nowadays. Boat trips, gold panning and accommodation: *Café Ahkuntupa | mid June–mid Sept daily | Njurguilahti, 45 km (28 mi) south of Inari | tel. 040 7 55 43 06 | www. ahkuntupa.fi*

URHO KEKKONEN NATIONAL PARK
(131 E4) (*F4*)
This huge park (980 mi²) on the Russian border is named after Urho Kekkonen, a passionate hiker, who was President of Finland for 25 years. Information about the park and keys for cabins in the wilderness can be obtained at the *Koilliskaira Visitor Centre (Tankavaarantie 11B | tel. 0205 64 72 51)*. Hiking and cross-country ski trails in the fells start from here and from the *Fell Centre Kiilopää (Kiilopääntie 620, Saariselkä | tel. 016 6 70 07 00 | www.kiilopaa.fi)*.

UTSJOKI (131 D2) (*F2*)
Half of the 1300 people who live in this, the northern-most settlement in Finland, are Sami. The villages of the native inhabitants are located on the banks of the rivers *Utsjoki* and *Tenojoki*. The latter is one of the richest salmon fishing grounds in Europe. If you take a trip along the Tenojoki, you can climb up the Sami's sacred mountain, *Ailigas* (620 m, 2034 ft) along the way and visit Finland's largest spring, *Sulaoja*. This is where a 63 km-long (39 mi) hiking trail starts, taking you through a spectacular canyon in the Kevo Nature Reserve that is 40 km-long (25 mi) and 80m deep. It is possible to tackle shorter sections, too.

Info: *Nature Information Hut | mid June–end Sept | Miessipolku 2 | tel. 0205 64 77 92*. *Giisa Village Hut* runs a café and sells reindeer meat and handicrafts *(Utsjoentie 9)*. Accommodation: *Hotel Luossajohda (22 rooms, 4 flats | Luossatie 4 | tel. 040 517 3178 | www.luossajohka.fi | Moderate)*.

ROVANIEMI

(129 D1) (*E6*) **Rovaniemi (pop. 60,000) is a lively place by Lappish standards.**
The capital of Lapland is a busy commercial centre with a corresponding infrastructure and airport. It is idyllically located at the confluence of the River Kemijoki and its tributary, the Ounasjoki. The architecture is sobre and functional. 90 percent of the old wooden town was destroyed following the explosion of a German Army ammunition train in 1944 which unleashed a huge fireball.

★ **Siida Sámi Museum**
Sami culture from the past to the present → p. 89

★ **Boat trips on the Lemmenjoki**
Up-river in a long boat through an untamed fluvial landscape → p. 90

★ **Arktikum**
The history of the northern people and their natural surroundings in an award-winning building → p. 92

★ **Kilpisjärvi**
A small Sami village and Finland's highest mountain → p. 93

MARCO POLO HIGHLIGHTS

SIGHTSEEING

ARKTIKUM ⭐ ●
A tubular glass complex and two partially subterranean buildings make up this award-winning centre that houses exhibitions on the people and nature of the north and arctic explorations. A multi-vision show and mythical tales are held in the Northern Lights Theatre. *June–Aug and early Dec until mid Jan daily 10am–6pm, otherwise Tue–Sun 10am–6pm | 12 euros | Pohjoisranta 4 | www.arktikum.fi*

JOULUPUKIN PAJAKYLÄ (SANTA CLAUS VILLAGE)
It's Christmas 365 days a year in a small wooden village on the Arctic Circle. Pixies in pointed red hats work through mountains of mail in the post office while Father Christmas welcomes guests for a photo. You can also take a ride on a sledge through the snow pulled by reindeer or dogs, have a look at an exhibition about Christmas customs around the world. *June–Aug daily 10am–6pm, Sept–Nov and mid Jan–end May until 5pm, Dec–mid Jan daily 9am–7pm | www.santaclausvillage.info*

FOOD & DRINK

INSIDER TIP ▶ NILI
This atmospheric restaurant is furnished like a wooden cabin. The Lappish specialities on the menu are carefully and imaginatively prepared. *Daily | Valtakatu 20 | tel. 0400 36 96 69 | www.nili.fi | Moderate*

SKY OUNASVAARA ⚜
This hotel restaurant, with its white tablecloths and beautiful view over the town, is one of the best in Rovaniemi. *Juhanuskalliontie | tel. 016 32 34 00 | www.laplandhotels.com | Moderate*. The hotel *(Expensive)* has good accommodation and many of the 71 rooms have their own sauna.

WHERE TO STAY

BOREALIS B & B
Small, friendly place not far from the station. Good buffet breakfast, free Internet. *15 rooms | Asemieskatu 1 | tel. 016 3 42 01 30 | www.guesthouseborealis.com | Budget*

CLARION HOTEL SANTA CLAUS
A totally non-Christmasy, well equipped and centally located, modern hotel. Interesting special offers in the summer. *151 rooms | Korkalonkatu 29 | tel. 016 32 13 21 | www.hotelsantaclaus.fi | Moderate*

INFORMATION

ROVANIEMI TOURIST INFORMATION
Maakuntakatu 29–31, on Lordi Square | tel. 016 35 62 70 | www.visitrovaniemi.fi

LOW BUDGET

▶ In the *Pallas Yllästunturi National Park* hikers will find cabins in the middle of the wilderness where they can stay free of charge or for a small fee. There are ● free cabins that are not locked, and others for which you need a key and which cost 10 euros a night. Keys can be picked up at the *Yllästunturi Visitors' Centre* (advanced reservation necessary) *| tel. 0205 64 79 30 | www.outdoors.fi*

▶ *Outa,* a guesthouse in Rovaniemi, is a cheap alternative to Lapland's rather expensive larger hotels: slightly unconventional but cosy. Double rooms cost 60 euros. *7 rooms | Ukkoherrantie 16 | tel. 016 312 474 | www.guesthouseouta.com*

WHERE TO GO

INSIDER TIP AAVASAKSA
(128 C2) (*Ø E6*)

This partly rocky hill 10 km (6¼ mi) north of Ylitornio forms part of the Finnish 'national landscape'. There is a 🔭 viewing tower on the summit which provides simply stunning views as far as Sweden. Freshly grilled fish can be had 50 km (31 mi) down river in the *Café Myllyn Pirtti (Jun–Aug daily | Koskitie, Kukkola | Budget)* located at the Kukkola Rapids which is rich in fish and famous for its picturesque wooden jetties used by salmon fishers.

INSIDER TIP KEMI (128 C2) (*Ø E7*)

The biggest snow castle *(lumi linna)* in the world can be found every year between February and the beginning of April in Kemi, 120 km (74½ mi) away. Not only chilled drinks are to be had in this temporary structure, there is also a restaurant, a hotel and even a wedding chapel. And, of course, there is a sauna as well *(www.snowcastle. net)*. If that isn't cold enough for you, take a trip into the pack ice: the icebreaker *Sampo* cuts its way through sheets up to 5 ft thick. *(Dec–April | tel. 016 25 88 78 | www.sampotours.com | 4 hrs cost 240 euros, incl. food, guide and a swim between icebergs in a thermal suit).*

KILPISJÄRVI ★ (130 A3) (*Ø C3*)

The tiny Sami alpine village (pop. 100) in the northwest corner of Finland is surrounded by the highest mountains in the country. This is where Finland's oldest nature conservation area can be found and steps lead up sacred Mount *Saana* (1029 m, 3376 ft). Finland's highest mountain, *Halti* (1324 m, 4344 ft), is just 55 km (34 mi) away. Cabins and holiday flats can be rented from *Kilpisjärvi lomakeskus (Kasivarrentie 14188 | tel. 016 53 78 01 | Moderate)*. The *Café Restaurant Ida-Sofie* has a lovely

The Northern Lights, photographed in Pallas Yllästunturi National Park

view of Saana *(daily | Käsivarrentie 14205 | tel. 016 53 S77 90 | Moderate)*. Info: *www. kilpisjarvi.org*

PALLAS YLLÄSTUNTURI NATIONAL PARK
(130 C4) (*Ø D–E4*)

Finland's third largest national park is dominated by a 100 km-long (62 mi) eroded mountain range *(fjells)* that can be seen from everywhere. *Pallas Yllästunturi* is known for its very good infrastructure. There are three visitors' centres *(in Pallas, Enontekiö and Äkäslompolo);* hiking and cross-country ski trails of varying lengths and levels of difficulty are well signposted. The 55 km-long (34 mi) *Hetta Pallas Trail* in the northern part of the park is particularly popular. In winter, 500 km (310 mi) of cross-country ski trails are prepared. Info: *www.outdoors.fi/pallas-yllastunturinp*

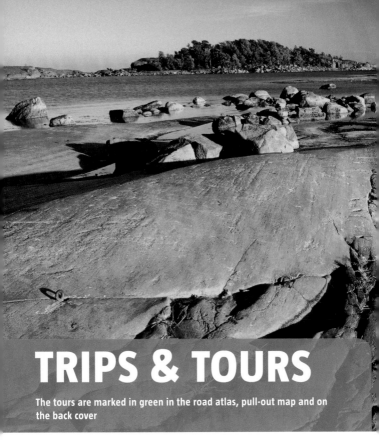

TRIPS & TOURS

The tours are marked in green in the road atlas, pull-out map and on the back cover

1

TOUR OF THE SKERRIES: ACROSS THE ISLANDS AND ALONG THE COAST

A tour of the skerries off Turku is a way to experience the wonders of nature and culture first hand. Take in the sea air, stay the night in fishermen's cabins and enjoy the lovely views either on the long, circular Archipelago Trail through the skerries (5–6 days, 260 km/162 mi) or the shorter route (3–4 days, 122 km/76 mi). Ferry route planning: *www.lautat.fi*. Addresses and detailed maps: *www.turkutouring.fi* and *www.saaristo.org*

The Archipelago Trail can, of course, be done by car, motorbike or even using public transport. However, the best way to explore the skerries is by bike – the conditions are perfect, the roads little used and quiet. Bikes can be rented all over the place. The Tourist Information Office in Turku is happy to put together an excursion package for you, including bikes, ferry tickets and accommodation. The circular Archipelago Trail through the skerries itself is well signposted, with eight ferries and twelve bridges linking the area southwest of Turku. In 2009, the island communities Iniö, Houtskari, Korppoo, Nauvo and Parainen amalgamated to form the mu-

Photo: Rocky landscape near Hanko

Finland means variety: from the skerries to the Arctic Ocean – here are three of the most beautiful tours

nicipality of Länsi-Turunmaa (Swedish: *Väståboland*).

From **Turku** → p. 60, you first head for **Kaarina** and then the ruins of the **bishops' castle** and the **manor house on Kuusisto** with its museum and café *(May–Aug Wed–Sat 11am–5pm | Linnanrauniontie 577 | www.nba.fi/en/kuusisto_manor)*. The turn off onto road 180 – the principal route along the Archipelago Trail – is in Kaarina.

From here, a very pretty road takes you from one island to the next. You will cross several bridges and have to make use of the (free) ferries. It is well worth staying in the Art Nouveau hotel, **Villa Rainer**, on the next island, **Kirjala**. It also has an award-winning restaurant *(4 rooms | Skråbbontie 244, Kirjala | tel. 02 4 58 90 77 | www.villa rainer.fi | Expensive)*. Apart from hardy islanders, Kirjala is also home to a local breed of sheep. Their breeders run the **Stentorp** sheep farm, idyllically situated on the sea, where they sell 😋 natural wool and leather products *(www.stentorp. parnet.fi)*. The next stop is in **Parainen**, a town surrounded by the sea on all sides. This gateway to the Turku skerries is known for the largest opencast limestone quarry in Finland. The Old Town district Vanha Malmi and the medieval greystone church are well worth a visit. On the way to the ferry from Lillmälo to Nauvo, stop at 😋 **Tupa summer café** *(June–Aug daily | Sattmark 1, Parainen | www.sattmark.fi)*. Henna Kallio serves homemade berry cake, freshly ground coffee and tea from fair-trade companies in a pretty former captain's house. Cabins for overnight stays are also available *(tel. 040 7 46 06 53 | Budget)*. The ferry from Parainen will take you to the harbour town of **Nauvo**. If you have enough time, you should take a boat trip to the lighthouse on the little island of **Utö**. The distinctive red and white build-ing has been warning ships out at sea for 200 years and is the oldest lighthouse in the country still in operation. Another ferry and – following the long Archipelago Trail route – will bring you to **Korppoo**, a popular holiday resort. Crafts, pottery and galleries can be found in the village cen-tre and a lovely view is to be had from 🔭 **Solateria** lookout tower on Ruman beach. The next ferry is not far away: from neigh-boring **Galtby** the journey continues to the north and the island community of **Houtskari** (Swedish: *Houtskär*). This is the only Swedish-speaking island in this group of skerries.

The ferry (not free) to Dalen on **Iniö** takes an hour. The little community, which in-corporates more than 1000 islands, has a shoreline of 700 km (435 mi) and is worth seeing in its own right, especially the idyllic countryside around the settlement, the stone church and the nature trail. This leads to a 40m-high cliff, on top of which is a 🔭 wooden lookout point. From here,

English landscape garden meets palatial Italian architecture: Louhisaari Manor

there is a view over the sea of skerries to the mainland. Further north is the **Kustavi** archipelago, named after King Gustav III. At this, the furthest outpost in the skerries, you are very close to the Åland Islands. The community lives from the summer tourist trade; there is a lively marina and lot of restaurants and crafts people. The **Laura Peterzens Café** *(closed Sat/Sun | Parattulan Rantatie 461 | www.cafelaura. psu.edu)* is particularly lovely. You can spend the night in one of the six summerhouses on the harbour *(Vuosnaisten Meriasema | tel. 02 87 75 12 | www.vuosna istenmeriasema.com | Budget)*.

On the return journey along the circular route to Turku, you pass the little fishing community of **Taivassalo** with pretty Pyhän Ristin Church. **Louhisaari Manor**, in Askainen, is just round the corner. This grand building is a rare example of Late Renaissance architecture in Finland *(mid May–end Aug daily 11am–5pm | 5 euros | Louhisaarentie 244 | www.nba.fi/en/louhi saari_manor)*.

If you choose the shorter Archipelago Trail, there are some differences to the route. Take the ferry from Nauvo to Hanka and follow the twisty road across the island of Rymättylä to Naantali. You can take another short-cut by using the ferry from Mossala to Röölä on Rymättylä.

2 IN FINLAND'S LAKE DISTRICT: PADDLING WITH A VIEW

One of the oldest and lovliest canoe tours is the Wanhan-Witosen paddle trail from Petäjävesi to Arvaja on Lake Päijänne. It will take you along narrow, twisty stretches of water and across open lakes through the wilderness and Finland's cultural landscape. The whole route is 75 km (46½ mi) long and takes 3–5 days, although shorter sections can also be tackled.

You don't have your own canoe? No problem. Boats, including maps and other equipment, instruction (20–25 euros/day) and transport (20 euros/day) can all be organised for you by **Kieväri Rantapirtti**. Supervision on the first day, for example, costs around 40 euros/hr *(Petäjävedentie 447, Koskenpää | tel. 0400 32 38 54 | www. kp-rantapirtti.fi)*. If you want to book a guided tour, contact **Tauno Pajunen** *(Vaivaroistentie 38, Jämsä | tel. 0400 20 30 51 | www.retkiluistelu.com)* or **Tavinsulka Canoetours** *(tel. 0400 89 92 80 | www. tavinsulka.com)*. There are a total of 19 landing places along the whole length of the route where you can camp, cook and have a rest. These are marked clearly on a waterproof map of the tour, as are rapids, places to stay and other important pieces of information. Maps are available from the Tourist Information Office in Jämsä *(Mon–Fri 9am–4pm | Seppolantie 5 | tel. 020 6 38 24 51 | matkailu.jamsek.fi/ en/wanhawitonen)*. 4 of a total of 8 largish rapids can easily be tackled in summer when the level of the water is low. The not-so-brave can either have a look at the rapids from the bank or walk around the most difficult passages *(Kalliokoski, Survostenkoski* and *Myllykoski)*. Trailers for transporting canoes can be found in several places.

The tour begins in the village of **Petäjävesi** → p. 68 from the Kirveslahti jetty. After just a few hundred metres you will want to stop to take a look at the old wooden church in Petäjävesi itself – just like Finns have done for more than 200 years. Even today, wedding parties often leave on a church boat. It you don't want to spend the night on this lonely headland, you'll have to paddle another 18 km (11 mi) and navigate three rapids before finding a comfortable bed, a sauna and a hearty meal near Kieväri Rantapirtti (see above). The next day, the route follows the banks of **Lake Iso-Rautavesi** to the narrow **Luomenjoki** river that leads into **Lake Pirttijärvi**. This stretch includes the most difficult rapids. After a good 16 km (10 mi) you will reach your next stop for the night, for which you will need a sleeping bag and a tent.

On the third day you will be paddling down the narrow **Lahnajärvi** until you reach the **Rasuaniemi** peninsula on Lake Kankarisvesi. A landscape painting of this area by Eliel Saarinen used to grace the old Finnish 5-mark note *(witonen)* and gave this paddle tour its name. Now you have almost reached **Jämsänkoski**, where many paddlers finish their tours. You can spend the night on the idyllic headland in **Kotkanpesä** campsite *(Koskenpääntie 383 | tel. 0440 22 42 22 | www.kotkanpesa.eu | Budget)* or in the **Mataran Puuro ja Peti B & B** *(8 rooms | Koskenpääntie 97 | tel. 040 5 65 35 23 | www.mataranpuurojapeti. fi | Budget)*.

If you want to continue to **Päijänne**, your equipment needs to be transported to the next starting point – Tauno Pajunen can organise this for you (see above). The last part of this route is along the quite River **Jämsänjoki** as far as **Hulkkionlahti Bay**, where the tour finishes. If you want to stay another night, lovely accommodation can be found at the **berry winery Uusi-Yijälä** with its lakeside restaurant Patapirtti *(5 rooms | Jyväskyläntie 808, Jämsä | tel. 045 6 51 14 05 | www.patapirtti.fi | Moderate)*.

3 FROM THE ARCTIC CIRCLE TO THE ARCTIC OCEAN

It's going to get lonely: always heading northwards, this journey will take you through uninhabited countryside as far as the Arctic Ocean. *En route* you will cross national parks, Sami territory, gold digger country and meet the odd reindeer. Total length of route: 500 km (310 mi).

Rovaniemi → p. 91 is the gateway to Lapland. Allow yourself one or two days

The building could not have been better designed: the Arktikum in Rovaniemi

in the capital of this northern-most province and pay a visit to the **Arktikum** before heading off into the wild expanse of Lapland. The centre provides in-depth information on the culture of the people of the Arctic and life north of the Arctic Circle.

From Rovaniemi, the route takes you almost in a straight line northwards to the Arctic Ocean. Just a little off the main route is **Pyhä-Luosto National Park** – a wild, romantic area crossed by a 35km-long (22mi) moutain range. All sorts of summer and winter sports are available in the holiday centre in Luosto nearby *(www.laplandluosto.fi)*, and you can even dig for your own lucky amethyst if you take a trip to the only amethyst mine still in operation in Finland *(www.amethystmine.fi)*. *Hotel Aurora Chalet (28 rooms | Luppokeino 1 , Luosto | 016 3 27 27 00 | www.aurorachalet.fi | Moderate)* is a perfect place to stay in the national park.

From Luosto, take the road to Aska and travel a good 100 km (62 mi) to the north to **Tankavaara.** In the early 20th century this was the centre of the Finnish Gold Rush. There are still some optimists here looking for that big nugget. A visit is well worthwhile just to grasp what makes these treasure hunters carry on. Pay a visit to Europe's only gold museum or pan for the precious metal yourself – it's great fun even if the bowl is empty in the end *(www.tankavaara.fi)*!

From here, it's not far to **Urho Kekkonen National Park** → **p. 91**, where eagles, wolves and bears still live. From ❄ **Kaunispää,** a 438m-high (1437 ft) fell on the edge of the park, there is a magnificent view of the surrounding countryside. 100 km (62 mi) further on, an enormous stretch of water appears in the middle of this deserted region. Lake Inari covers 540 mi² and is Finland's third largest lake. The Sami people consider the lake sacred and there are several ritual sites on its banks and on the islands. You approach the water and its myths from **Inari** → **p. 88**.

If you are travelling in summer, you may not want to go to sleep at all at night but to be outside all the time. The bright nights are silvery and have a magical feel. Why not drive the last 170 km (106 mi) by night? Past the Tenojoki, rich in salmon, and the little settlement **Utsjoki** → **p. 91** on its banks, with perhaps a detour to the spectacular gorges of the **Kevo Nature Reserve** *(Nature Information Hut | Miessipolku 2, Utsjoki | tel. 0205 64 77 92)*, you will reach the northern-most point of Finland. **Nuorgam** is the name of the last village you pass in the north. Nowhere else in Finland are the summer nights so bright and the winter days so dark as here in this little settlement that is home to just 250 people. Most of the residents are Sami who make a living from fishing and reindeer farming. The Norwegian border is just a few minutes drive from here – and in one hour you will reach the Arctic Ocean.

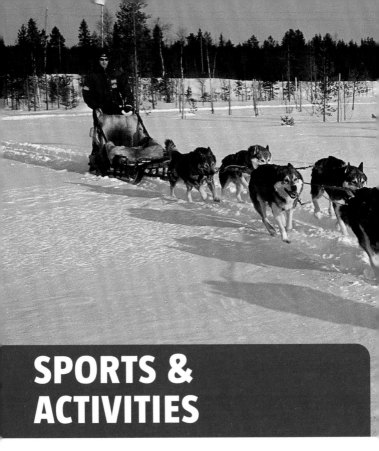

SPORTS & ACTIVITIES

Finland is a nation of sports-lovers. It may only have a population of 5 million, but when you see how often Finns end up on the winners' podium at international sports events you think the country must have at least 50 million inhabitants.

The success of Finnish top athletes is an indication of the huge enthusiasm that everyone in the country shares for sport. Every fifth Finn is a member of a sports club. Winter sports – for obvious reasons – are particularly well represented. It is perfectly normal for Finns to feel totally at home on skates or skies. This is why it is not football that is the king of sports, but ice hockey. No other kind of sport gets the

Finns as emotionally involved as ice hockey. Only motor sports reach a similar level of popularity. Whether cross-country skiing or aerobics, golf or the triathlon: whatever sport you want to do the Finns will be with you all the way. That couldn't really be any different in a nation of people who go out jogging when it is minus 25 °C (-13 °F)!

BICYCLES & MTBS

Cycling is very popular. Larger towns often have a good network of cycle paths. Major roads are less suitable for cyclists as there are generally no cycle lanes or wide hard shoulders. Long tours are best planned

A sports-lover's perfect holiday: Finland's forests and lakes offer everything to make your heart beat faster

on minor roads. Cycle maps and tour guides can be found online under *www. karttakauppa.fi*. Masses of suggested routes are listed under *www.pyoraillen suomessa.fi*. Bikes can easily be taken on district line services for 4–5 euros (except during rush hours 7am–9am and 3pm–6pm). Bikes must be booked one day in advance for transport on long-distance coaches and trains (10 euros a bike).

GOLF

The season may be short, but playing a round of golf during the long days in mid-summer on one of the 126 golf courses in Finland is an experience not to be forgotten. Half of them are 18-hole courses; most are also open to visitors from abroad. Green fees vary from 45 to 70 euros/day. In winter you can dress for the cold and go to the ice golf course at the *Arctic Golf Club* in Rovaniemi *(www.arcticgolf.net)* where coloured balls are used. There are 20 courses around Helsinki. One of the most beautiful is the *St Laurence Club* in Lohja *(www.stlg.fi)*. For a list of all greens and further information see: *Suomen Golfliitto | www.golf.fi*

FISHING & ICE FISHING

If you limit yourself to a short ice-fishing rod (called a 'pimpel rod' from the Swedish *pimpelfiske*), you don't need a fishing licence. If you are between 18 and 64 and use other equipment, you have to pay a *kalastuksenhoitomaksu* – a fishing ground conservation fee. At present this costs 7 euros/week or 22 euros/year. You also need a permit from the owner of the stretch of water *(viehekalastusmaksut)*. This can be obtained from the respective local authority for 7 euros/week or 29 euros/year. You can then try your luck for perch, pike, zander, trout and grayling. Special regulations apply on the Åland Islands. Information can be found under *www. visitfinland.com/fishing* or from the Finnish Federation for Recreational Fishing: *www. vapaa-ajankalastaja.fi*.

HIKING

Ideal hiking conditions can be found in the 35 national parks and nine hiking areas with trails of varying degrees of difficulty and length, campfire sites and cabins. Everything is possible from a gentle stroll to a trekking tour. But you must be aware that you are a long way from any possible help: in addition to appropriate clothing and stout shoes you need a compass, maps, food, first-aid kit, mosquito spray and wet-weather gear in your rucksack. Information: *www.outdoors.fi, www.visit finland.com.* Maps: *www.excursionmap.fi*

ICE SWIMMING

Many hotels and holiday centres make holes in the ice for winter swimmers. Before you think: 'They must be mad, these Finns', try it yourself! *Avantounti*, as ice swimming is called here, gets your system going, puts you in a good mood and makes you feel great. On top of this, you'll sleep like a new-born baby afterwards. In winter, the INSIDER TIP *Rauhaniemi* public swimming area near Tampere is a lovely place to give it a try (on the shore of Lake Näsijärvi with a sauna). *Rauhaniementie 24 | 4.50 euros*

KAJAKING & CANOEING

The possibilities for exploring Finland's waterways by boat are sheer endless. A good overview of the most popular tours around the country can be found under *www.visitfinland.com*; for the Saimaa region *www.canoeinfinland.com* is the best address. Guided tours, rafting and equipment can be organised by tourist information offices (and under the addresses mentioned above). Rowing is a national pastime and a rowing boat belongs in every *mökki*. A traditional group phenomenon is church boat rowing in which up to 16 rowers paddle together in pairs. Lots of local rowing clubs have church boats to rent.

RIDING

The Finnish horse that was once used soley as a draught and working horse, is now a popular hack. Its docile temperament makes it as reliable as the famous Iceland pony. Trekking across the Finnish countryside is now gaining popularity and is available through the trekking association *(www.vaellustallit.fi/members.html)*. Addresses of local stables can be found in tourist information offices.

SAILING

Most sailing boats can be found around the Åland Islands and the major sailing centres Oulu, Pietarsaari, Rauma, Turku, Hanko, Loviisa, Kotka and Helsinki. There are also lovely sailing routes with lots of little marinas on the lakes. Tourist information offices can arrange boats and tours for you. If you are an adept sailor yourself, make sure you have up-to-date sea charts due to continuous land rise *(www.john-nurminenmarine.com)* and listen to the weather forecasts. Trips along the Saimaa Canal must be registered 14 days in advance *(www.fma.fi)*.

SLED SAFARIS

● A sled safaris with animals is an experience not to be forgotten. Reindeer safaris can only be found in Lapland; husky safaris in other regions of Finland, too. Special warm clothes are usually provided. Friendly guides who treat their animals well can be found for example at Harriniva near Muonio. A 5-hour husky safari costs 200 euros per person; a 3-hour reindeer safari 180 euros *(www.harriniva.fi)*. Hetta Huskies in Enontekiö (www.hettahuskies.com) or the reindeer park in Salla *(www.sallareindeerpark.fi)* can also be recommended.

WINTER SPORTS

The winter in Finland lasts the best part of half a year. The continental climate means it snows from November until May; the dry air however makes temperatures as low as minus 30 °C (-22 F) bearable. The most dense network of cross-country ski trails is in Kuopio *(www.kuopioinfo.fi)*, Lahti is a mekka for the Nordic disciplines *(www.lahti.fi.)*, the longest downhill pistes in Finland are in Ylläsjärvi *(www.yllas.fi)*. Kuusamo/Ruka is an eldorado for skiers where part of the 'Bear's Ring' cross-country track is prepared in winter (www.ruka.fi), as is the mountainous skiing area in Pyhä-Luosto National Park *(www.laplandluosto.fi)*. Ice surfing on frozen lakes is new and gaining popularity.

MTBikers on the move: there are plenty of forests for cyling in Finland

TRAVEL WITH KIDS

Travelling with children in Finland is uncomplicated. Highchairs, baby facilities, cots and play areas are everywhere.

HELSINKI & THE SOUTH COAST

KORKEASAARI ZOO (0)
The most northerly zoo in Europe has more than 150 species, including the very rare snow leopard. *May–Aug daily 10am–8pm, April /Sept 10am–6pm, Oct–March 10am–4pm | by boat from the Market Square | adults 10 euros, children 5 euros, under 6 yrs free | www.korkeasaari.fi*

LINNANMÄKI (0)
Amusement park with rides and outdoor stage. *Tivolikuja 1 | end April–mid Sept, in summer daily 11am–10pm | entrance fee: 18–35 euros | www.linnanmaki.fi*

SEALIFE (0)
Sharks, seahorses and other sea creatures. *Tivolitie 10 | near Linnanmäki | May–Aug daily 10am–8pm, otherwise Thu–Tue 10am–5pm, Wed 10am–8pm | adults 15 euros, children 10 euros, cheaper if booked online | www.sealife.fi*

HEUREKA – THE FINNISH SCIENCE CENTRE ● (126 C5) (*ØD E13*)
Feel, test, join in and experiment with things in the world around us. *Mon–Wed/Fri 10am–5pm, Thu 10am–8pm, Sat/Sun 10am–6pm | Tikkurila, Vantaa | teenagers and adults 16–28 euros, under 16 yrs 11–14 euros | www.heureka.fi*

THE WEST COAST

INSIDER TIP▶ HERRA HAKKARAISEN TALO (126 A4) (*ØD D12*)
In the sleepwalker Mr. Clutterbuck's house, children enter the very Finnish fantasy world of the author Mauri Kunnas. *Mon–Fri 10am–5pm, Sept–May Sat 10am–2pm, June–Aug Sat 10am–4pm, Sun noon–4pm | Marttilankatu 10, Vammala | adults/children 5 euros, small children free | www.herrahakkaraisentalo.net*

KURALAN KYLÄMÄKI (124 C4) (*ØD D13*)
The 'Village of Living History' is based around a farmhouse from the 1950s. Depending on the weekly theme, children can feed the animals, harvest hay or make soap. *July–mid Sept Tue–Sun 10am–6pm |*

Have fun: the best recreation parks, museums, zoos and attractions in Finland for big and small

Jaanintie 45, Turku | adults 7.50, children 4.50 euros | www.turku.fi/museo

MOOMIN WORLD (124 B4) (*ш C13*)
Disneyland in Finnish: on an island off Naantali you can get to meet life-sized Moomins. *June–mid Aug daily 10am–6pm, end Aug noon–6pm, Feb 11am–5pm | Tuulensuunkatu 14, Naantali | 22 euros | www.muumimaailma.fi*

INSIDER TIP KIERIKKI STONE AGE CENTRE (128 D3) (*ш E8*)
Children can whet stones, paddle in a dug-out and learn how to build a trap. *Tue–Fri 10am–4pm, Sat noon–4pm | adults 8, children 7 euros, under 5 yrs free | Pahkalantie 447, Yli-Ii | www.kierikki.fi*

WASALANDIA (125 F1) (*ш C10*)
Zoom down the whitewater channel in a dug-out, do twirls in the air from a huge trampoline, or have fun on the climbing wall, in crocodile boats and in the tube labyrinth. *June daily 11am–5pm, July 11am–7pm, Aug sometimes only until 5pm | Vaskiluoto, Vaasa | adults 20 euros, children 15 euros | www.wasalandia.fi*

FINNISH LAKE DISTRICT

INSIDER TIP HIEKKALINNA (127 E4) (*ш G12*)
Every year artists build a huge sandcastle in Lappeenranta with a theatre, hut village and a merry-go-round. *June–Aug | www.hiekkalinna.lappeenranta.fi*

MOOMINVALLEY (126 B3) (*ш D12*)
Meet Moomin, the Snork Maiden and all the other creatures. *Tue–Fri 9am–5pm, Sat/Sun 10am–6pm | Hämeenpuisto 20, Tampere | adults 7 euros, children 2 euros | www.tampere.fi/muumi*

FESTIVALS & EVENTS

Detailed information about these and other events can be found under: *www.festivals.fi*

PUBLIC HOLIDAYS

1 Jan *Uusi vuosi* New Year's Day; **6 Jan** *Loppiainen* Epiphany/Russian Orthodox Christmas; **Good Friday** *Pitkäperjantai*; **Easter** *Pääsiäinen*; **1 May** *Vappu* May Day, Workers Day; **Ascension Day** *Helatorstai*; **Whitsun** *Helluntai*; **Fri/Sat after 20 June** *Juhannus* Midsummer celebrations; **6 Dec** *Itsenäisyyspäivä* Independence Day; **24–26 Dec** *Joulu* Christmas

FESTIVALS & EVENTS

FEBRUARY/MARCH

▶ *Musica nova* (Helsinki): This important European contemporary music festival lasts 2 weeks. *www.musicanova.fi*
▶ *Oulu Music Festival:* Classical music far in the north. *www.oulunmusiikkijuhlat.fi*

APRIL

▶ *Espoo April Jazz:* One week of big international names. *www.apriljazz.fi*

▶ *Tanssivirtaa Tampere:* Contemporary Finnish dance. *www.tanssivirtaa.net*

MAY

▶ *Vaasa Choir Festival:* Finnish choirs, from barbershop to opera. *www.vaasa.fi/choirfestival*

JUNE

▶ *Kuopio International Dance Festival:* One of the most important of its kind in northern Europe. *www.kuopiodancefestival.fi*,
▶ *Sodankylä Midnight Sun Film Festival:* Watch films under the midnight sun. *www.msfilmfestival.fi*, ▶ *Avanti! Summer Sounds:* Classical music in the old wooden town of Porvoo. *www.avantimusic.fi*,
▶ *Korsholm Music Festival:* Chamber music in unique settings on the islands around Korsholm/Vaasa. *www.korsholmmusicfestival.fi*, ▶ *Midsummer celebrations:* Parties everywhere with bonfires, dancing outside, ancient traditions. In Helsinki celebrations are held on Seurasaari Island *(see p. 36)*.

JULY

▶ *Eukonkanto:* The Wife Carrying World Championships are held every year in

Whenever the Finns get a bit lonely, they organise a party. And if they don't have any particular reason, they simply invent one

Sonkajärvi – one of Finland's more bizarre competitions. *www.eukonkanto.fi/en*

▶● *Seinäjoki Tango Festival:* Tango takes to the streets. *www.tangomarkkinat.fi*

▶ INSIDER TIP *Kuningasjätkä Tukkislaiskisat:* Acrobatics on logs at the rafters' championships near Ruka. *www.tukkilaiset.com*

▶ *Kuhmo Chamber Music Festival:* Talented musicians perform in the wilderness in East Finland. *www.kuhmofestival.fi*

▶ *Kaustinen Folk Musik Festival* The largest and oldest of its kind in the north. *www.kaustinen.net*

▶ *Ilosaarirock Joensuu:* One of the largest rock events with five stages. The 21,000 tickets are always sold out long in advance. *www.ilosaarirock.fi*

▶ *Pori Jazz:* 15,000 jazz-lovers listen to artists of world renown. *www.porijazz.fi*

▶ ⭐ *Savonlinna Opera Festival:* World class performances in a wonderful castle setting. *www.operafestival.fi*

AUGUST

▶ *Tampere International Theater Festival:* Showcasing the best Finnish and international theatre productions. *www.teatterikesa.fi*, ▶ *Helsinki Festival:* Three weeks of events incl. the 'Night of the Arts'. *www.helsinkifestival.fi*

SEPTEMBER

▶ *Lahti Int. Sibelius Festival:* Small, ambitious series of concerts devoted entirely to the great master. *www.sinfonialahti.fi*

NOVEMBER

▶ *Tampere Jazz Happening:* Free jazz, rock and world music. *www.tampere.fi/jazz*

DECEMBER

Christmas markets in Helsinki: ▶ *Thomas Market* (Esplanade Park), ▶ *Ladies' Bazaar* (Wanha Satama), ▶ *Arts and Crafts* (Old Student House). Information: *www.hel.fi*

LINKS, BLOGS, APPS & MORE

LINKS

▶ http://www.luontoportti.com/suomi/en The natural scents, sounds and sights in the countryside in Finland are everywhere – and often one is left standing in amazement without knowing what things are. NatureGate enables you to find fascinating information about hundreds of species of plants, birds, butterflies,

fish and landscape features together with thousands of superb images by top photographers.

▶ www.museot.fi/en.php Very practical: 925 museums are presented here with brief descriptions, addresses, exhibition calendars and opening times which can be looked up by theme, period or region

▶ aurora.fmi.fi/public_service Auroras Now! Is a service which helps those wanting to see the Northern Lights in Finland. The site operated by the Finnish Meteorological Institute (FMI) lets you know when the atmospheric conditions are best. If you don't want to miss this spectacle you can subscribe by sending a mail to: aurorasnow-feed@posti.fmi.fi. You will then receive a message when magnetic activity promises an unforgettable sight

▶ www.homelink.org Many Finns use social networks to exchange homes for holidays. The private houses and flats on offer are usually in major towns such as Helsinki, Turku, Lahti, Jyväskylä or Kuopio

VIDEOS & STREAMS

▶ wildbrownbear.fi/bearcam Finland is bear country. Live cams have been installed near the Russian border to capture bears on film in the evening and at night. Alternatively, you can browse the archives at other times

▶ www.natureit.net/kamera Have the young hatched yet? The cameras

set up by the University of Turku keep an eye on nests such as that of an osprey on the west coast of Finland

▶ www.yle.fi/elavaarkisto/haku/#/kategoria/Maakunnat Historic videos about Finland from the film archives of the Finnish TV broadcasting company YLE. Even without any knowledge of the language, many of the videos make exciting watching

▶ www.youtube.com/watch?v=rXPPcQ-UliA A French film providing a fascinating portrait of the Finnish sculptor Olavi Lanu who creates works in the shape of humans together with atmospheric pictures of the Finnish landscape

BLOGS

▶ www.finlandforthought.net An American in Finland – a clash of cultures is inevitable. Phil Schwarzmann from the USA never ceases to be amazed by Finland, the country he has chosen to live in, whether it's the sense of humour, Finnish habits and behaviour or political mannerisms. His blog provides witty, satirical commentaries, video clips and background information

▶ www.expat-blog.com/en/directory/europe/finland As its name suggests, these are blogs written by all sorts of native English speakers living in or travelling to Finland

APPS

▶ Hei Finland If 'Kaunis ilma tänään' doesn't mean a lot to you, then 'Hei Finland' may help you. With this app you can learn Finnish through 100 everyday expressions and listen to their pronunciation

▶ Finland: Business Traveler's Passport Perfect for those in Finland on business, although many of the tips can be used when on holiday there, too

TRAVEL TIPS

ARRIVAL

✈ Most people visiting Finland will probably want to fly. There are direct flights from most international airports in the UK to a number of different destinations in Finland (Helsinki, Turku, Oulo, Rovaniemi and Tampere, among others). Regular flights are operated by national airlines such as British Airways (www.britishairways.com) and Finnair (www.finnair.com), as well as by budget airlines which often fly to less well-known destinations. For all flights, including those from the USA and Ireland, it is worth spending some time comparing prices on the Internet. A flight from the UK to Helsinki takes approx. 4hrs. Inland flights from Helsinki operate to 27 different domestic airports. Finnair runs shuttlebuses from all Finnish airports into the centre of the respective town or city (price: 5–6 euros). At Helsinki, the bus line 615 (4 euros) links the airport with the centre; bus no. 61 will take you to Tikkurila station. A shared taxi costs 24–27 euros (travel time approx. 35 min).

🚢 If you want to take you own car, ferries operate from mainland Europe to Helsinki (eg. from Travemünde with Finnline or from Rostock or Stockholm with the Silja Line). All ferry connections – including combinations of ferry crossing and air travel – can be found under www.ferrycenter.fi. For those touring Scandinavia as a whole, Finland can be reached by travelling up the east coast of Sweden or by taking the more picturesque route up the Norwegian coast.

🚆 Rail connections to Finland are via Copenhagen and Stockholm, and then by ferry to Turku or from Kapellskär to Naantali.

BANKS & MONEY

The local currency is the euro. Payment with a credit or debit card is commonplace. Money can be withdrawn from cash dispensers using an EC card without any problem. Exchange bureaus can be found in airports, stations and in major cities. As all prices in Finland are rounded off to the nearest 5 cents, there are no 1 or 2 cent coins in circulation. Should you come across such Finnish coins, hang on to them – these rare coins are much sought after.

BREAKDOWN SERVICE

The automobile association Autoliitto, similar to the AA and RAC, has a 24-hour breakdown service which extends to cars registered outside Finland: tel. 0200 80 80 | www.autoliitto.fi

RESPONSIBLE TRAVEL

It doesn't take a lot to be environmentally friendly whilst travelling. Don't just think about your carbon footprint whilst flying to and from your holiday destination but also about how you can protect nature and culture abroad. As a tourist it is especially important to respect nature, look out for local products, cycle instead of driving, save water and much more. If you would like to find out more about eco-tourism please visit: www.ecotourism.org

From arrival to weather

Holiday from start to finish: the most important addresses and information for your Finland trip

CAR HIRE

International and local car hire companies can be found in every town. Demand for mobile homes (RVs) is strong is July and should be booked well in advance. In general, prices are a little higher than in the rest of Europe. Slightly cheaper offers can be found from private individuals under *www.budget.fi* and *www.irent.fi*. Due to the long distances, be careful about free mileage limits. Manuals in English are advisable (especially for mobile homes).

CUSTOMS

EU residents can bring goods for their personal use with them without paying duty as long as certain quantities are not exceeded. In the case of cigarettes which do not have a health warning in Finnish or Swedish, this is 200 cigarettes, 50 cigars, 250g pipe tabacco. Info: *www.tulli.fi*. Duty/tax free allowances for the UK for example can be found under: *www.heathrow-airport-guide.co.uk/dutyfree.html*

DOGS

Dogs need a pet passport (PETS), have to be chipped, and must be dewormed during the month before departure. In most places, dogs must be kept on the lead; there are many fenced-in dog parks for them the run about and meet other dogs. Most of the larger hotels have rooms for dog owners but many owners of summer-houses do not accept pets. The number of cabins on ferries in which dogs can also travel is limited. Dogs are not allowed at many tourist attractions, in restaurants or on beaches.

BUDGETING

Coffee	90 cents– 2.50 euros *for a cup of coffee*
Train ticket	approx. 72 euros *for a trip from Helsinki to Oulu (612 km/380mi)*
Beer	4–5 euros *for half a litre in a pub*
Bus ticket	approx. 23 euros *for a trip from Kuopio to Jyväskylä (144 km/90mi)*
Petrol	approx. 1.60 euros *for 1 litre*
Chocolate	1.85 euros *for a bar of Fazer chocolate*

DRIVING IN FINLAND

Finland has an excellent road network. You drive on the right and seatbelts must be worn both in the front and the back. You must always drive with dipped headlights on. The legal drink-driving limit is 0.5%. The speed limit in build-up areas is 50 km/h (30 mph) and 80–100 km/h (50–62 mph) outside. On dual carriageways and motorways (longer stretches are only to be found in the south of Finland), the speed limit is 120 km/h (75 mph). Keep within these limits – there are countless speed enforcement cameras. Basically speaking, give way to traffic coming from the right – this applies to roundabouts, too. Buses moving off and trams always have right of way.

The petrol station network in Finland is good. These are often in combination with a café, snack bar and grocery store. Automatic petrol pumps, with instructions in several languages, which can be used 24-hrs a day are commonplace and take standard credit cards. There are fewer petrol stations in the north of Finland and Lapland. You should plan your journey carefully (summary of petrol stations and garages: *www.abcasemat.fi, www.teboil.fi, www.neste.fi*). If you plan travelling long distances by car in winter, make sure that you have snow chains, a shovel, a tow rope, jumper leads, a sack of sand, blankets and a spirit of adventure with you.

ELECTRICITY

230 volt. Visitors from the UK will need an adapter to fit the standard European plug.

EMBASSIES & CONSULATES

BRITISH EMBASSY
Itäinen Puistotie 17 | 00140 Helsinki | tel.: (358) 9 22 86 51 00 | ukinfinland.fco.gov.uk

EMBASSY OF CANADA
Pohjoisesplanadi 25 B | 00140 Helsinki | tel.: (358) 9 22 85 30 | www.canadainternational.gc.ca/finland-finlande

EMBASSY OF IRELAND
Erottajankatu 7 A | 00130 Helsinki | tel.: (358) 96 82 42 40 | www.irishembassy.fi

EMBASSY OF THE UNITED STATES
Itäinen Puistotie 14 B | 00140 Helsinki | tel.: (358) 9 61 62 50 | finland.usembassy.gov

EMERGENCY SERVICES

For emergency services dial *112*. Road accidents must be registered with the central Finnish vehicle insurance office which handles accidents with non-Finnish cars. *Tel.: 040 4 50 45 10 | www.liikennevakuutuskeskus.fi*

HEALTH

Medical care in Finland is of a very high standard even in areas some way from larger towns. Check with your insurance company before departure as to how payment is to be handled in Finland and make sure you take a European Health Insurance Card (EHIC) with you.

INFORMATION

Having closed its offices abroad, the Finnish Tourist Board can only be contacted outside the country via its tourist portal *www.visitfinland.com*. The information shown (also in English) is regularly updated.
The Finnish Tourist Board works in close cooperation with and for the Finnish travel industry, implementing and financing marketing projects with industry, and aims at developing more enticing, competitive products for visitors to Finland.

INTERNET

Finland has the highest number of internet connections per capita worldwide. The Finnish mobile phone network is nationwide. Despite this, should you find that your summerhouse is in a dead spot, normally a short walk up the hill will solve the problem.

LANGUAGE

For foreigners, understanding Finnish is impossible. Only in the case of imported words such as *posti* or *grillikioski* can you work out what it means. Beyond that, it's merely guesswork. Finnish belongs to the Finno-Ugric family of languages which is totally different from any other. But don't worry: many Finns speak good English.

MEDIA

International papers are available at the airport and at stations in larger towns. Some English magazines can be found in *kioski*, in bookshops and in some supermarkets. The *Helsinki Times* is published on Thursdays and is available at kiosks and bookshops or online under *www.helsinkitimes.fi*. Finland's most widely read daily newspaper, the *Helsingin Sanomat,* also has articles in English under *www.hs.fi/english*. The Finnish TV channel *Yle* broadcasts news in English Mon–Fri at 11am and has news in brief online under *www.yle.fi/uutiset/news*.

MOSQUITOS & CO.

Called *ötökkä* in Finnish, mosquitos are a real menace and are inextricably part of the Finnish summer. Insect repellents and antidotes are available locally from chemists and similar shops. Mosquito coils help make an evening on the lake more enjoyable; the locals in Lapland even sometimes wear a kind of beekeepers' hat with a veil over their faces. Ticks can be found south of a line from Oulu to Joensuu, although the only risk of borreliosis or meningitis is in Åland and along the west coast as far as Oulu. The fox tapeworm does not exist in Finland which means you can pick berries and mushrooms without needing to worry.

OPENING TIMES

Supermarkets are generally open from Mon–Fri 9am–9pm and Sat 9am–6pm. In December as well as mid June–mid August also on Sun noon–9pm. Small businesses have their own very individual

CURRENCY CONVERTER

£	€	€	£
1	1.10	1	0.90
3	3.30	3	2.70
5	5.50	5	4.50
13	14.30	13	11.70
40	44	40	36
75	82.50	75	67.50
120	132	120	108
250	275	250	225
500	550	500	450

$	€	€	$
1	0.70	1	1.40
3	2.10	3	4.20
5	3.50	5	7
13	9.10	13	18.20
40	28	40	56
75	52.50	75	105
120	84	120	168
250	175	250	350
500	350	500	700

For current exchange rates see www.xe.com

times. Banks are usually open from 10am–4pm. Museums and tourist attractions sometimes change their opening times radically according to the season. It is always better to contact the tourist information office or check online. Most *kioski* are open until 8pm, some until 11pm, *ABC service stations* 24 hrs, also at weekends.

PASSPORTS & VISAS

A valid passport but no visa is necessary for EU citizens. For Americans, Canadians and Australians: to enter Finland, a passport but no visa is required for stays of up to three months.

PHONES & MOBILE PHONES

The international country code for Finland is 0 03 58. From abroad the 0 in the Finnish area code is omitted but has to be dialed for inland calls. The country code for the UK is 00 44, for Ireland 0 03 53, USA and Canada 001.

There are no public telephone boxes in Finland as everything is covered by the mobile phone network. Finnish prepaid cards can be bought at *kioski*, at garages and in *Sonera, Saunalahti, DNA, Elisa* and *Tele-Finland* shops. Another possibility is a rechargeable international SIM card. No roaming fees are liable if you use this and the card can be used again in another country.

POST

Post offices are open Mon–Fri 9am–6pm (*www.posti.fi*). A letter within Europe costs 80 cents; 65 cents for a postcard. Stamps are available from post offices or *kioski*, in bookshops, hotels and in stations. In the country, supermarkets often run the postal service which means that the opening hours are the same as the shop.

PRICES

As everywhere else in Scandinavia, the cost of living in Finland is higher than in Western Europe. Fruit and vegetables cost considerably more, for example, as they are largely imported or grown in the country at greater expense. Alcohol in Finland is much more expensive than in England. It is worth looking for special offers online before staying in a hotel.

PUBLIC TRANSPORT

Finland can be explored very easily by train. Even Lapland can be reached by overnight train via Oulu. The Finrail Pass allows unlimited travel on 3, 5 or 10 days in a month. Timetables and tickets under: *www.vr.fi*. Long-distance coaches also go to remote areas. They are cheap, fast and operate on almost 90 percent of roads. Check departure times and timetables beforehand, as there is seldom any information at remote bus stops: *www.mat kahuolto.fi, journey.fi/search/en/, www. expressbus.com*.

REDUCTIONS

In the summer, many hotels have reduced prices – always ask for reductions and special offers before checking-in. In addition, lots of hotels cooperate with one each other and have introduced a reduced-price system. The 'Travel & Stay Cheque' system, *Finncheque*, for example, is valid for 140 hotels scattered all over the country: *www.finncheque.com*. The *Helsinki Card* allows you free entrance to 60 museums and free travel on the capital's local transport system. Depending on the validity period *(24, 48 or 72 hrs)* it costs *31, 42 or 52 euros*. The *Turku Card (24 hrs./21 euros, 48 hrs./28 euros)* similarly provides free entrance to museums and free travel on buses in Turku.

TIME

Finland lies within the Eastern European time zone which is 2 hours ahead of Greenwich Mean Time. It is 7 hours behind Eastern Standard Time and 10 hours behind Pacific Standard Time.

WEATHER & CLIMATE

Finland has a continental climate which means Arctic temperatures in winter (as low as -40° C, -40° F) and warm to hot days in summer (up to 30°C, 86° F), with water temperatures topping the 20°C (68° F) mark. As Finland is a Nordic country it is seldom muggy and when it rains and in the evenings it soon gets cold. Being so far north, the days in summer.

WHERE TO STAY

There are approx. 350 campsites in Finland, 200 of which belong to the Finnish Campingsite Association *(www.camping.fi)*. Reductions are available with a *Scandinavia Campingcard* (6 euros). Most campsites also have cabins (from 40 euros/day) or better equipped holiday houses (70–120 euros/day). Depending on the amenities, tents or caravans cost between 10–25 euros each per day, seldom more.

Mosts campsites have a sauna on the water and boats for hire

There are countless *mökkis* everywhere: simple cabins can be found under *www.luontoon.fi, www.villipohjola.fi,* classic holiday *mökkis* under *www.lomarengas.fi* and cottages directly from the owners under *www.huvila.net* or *www.fintouring.de.* Prices start at 300 euros to well over 1000 euros/week, depending on the location, time and furnishing.

The association ECEAT *(www.eceat.fi)* organises accommodation on 😊 organic farms. If you want to earn your board and lodging by helping out, then take a look at *www.wwoofinternational.org.*

Prices for B & B range from 30–70 euros for a double room.

WEATHER IN HELSINKI

	Jan	Feb	March	April	May	June	July	Aug	Sept	Oct	Nov	Dec
Daytime temperatures in °C/°F	-3/27	-4/25	0/32	6/43	13/55	19/66	22/72	20/68	15/59	8/46	4/39	0/32
Nighttime temperatures in °C/°F	-8/18	-9/16	-6/21	0/32	6/43	11/52	14/57	13/55	9/48	4/39	0/32	-4/25
Sunshine hours/day	1	2	5	6	8	10	9	7	5	3	1	1
Precipitation days/month	12	9	7	9	7	8	9	10	10	11	11	12
Water temperatures in °C/°F	1/34	1/34	1/34	2/36	5/41	11/52	16/61	16/61	13/55	9/48	5/41	3/37

USEFUL PHRASES FINNISH

PRONUNCIATION

Finnish is generally pronounced as it is written, but bear the following in mind:
'j' is like 'y' in 'yet', 'y' as a consonant is like the French vowel in 'tu', 'ä' is similar
to the 'e' in 'met'. Double vowels or consonants are twice as long as single ones –
this is important for avoiding misunderstandings (tuuli = wind, tuli = fire).
The stress is always on the first syllable of a word.

IN BRIEF

Yes/No/Maybe	Kyllä/Ei/Ehkä
Please/Thank you	Ole hyvä/Kiitos
Excuse me / Pardon?	Anteeksi / Anteeksi, kuinka?
May I ...?	Saanko ...
I would like to .../Have you got ...?	Haluaisin .../Onko teillä
How much is ...	Kuinka paljon maksaa ...?
I (don't) like that	Pidän siitä/En pidä siitä
good/bad/bad	hyvä/huono/paha
broken/doesn't work	rikki/se ei toimi
too much/much/little	liian paljon/paljon/vähän
all/nothing	kaikki/ei mitään
Help!/Attention!/Caution!	Apua!/Huomio!/Varokaa!
Ambulance	ambulanssi
Police/Fire brigade	poliisi/palokunta
Prohibition/forbidden	kielto/kielletty
danger/dangerous	vaara/vaarallinen
May I take a photo here/of you?	Saanko ottaa sinusta/teistä/täällä valokuvan?

GREETINGS, FAREWELL

Good morning!/afternoon!/ evening!/night!	Hyvää huomenta!/Hyvää päivää/ Hyvää iltaa!/hyvää yötä!
Hello!/Goodbye!	Hei, terve, Moi/näkemiin
See you	Heippa! Moikka! Moimoi.
My name is ...	Minun nimeni on ...
What's your name?	Mitä teidän nimenne on? Mitä sinun nimesi on?
I'm from ...	Minä olen ...

Puhutko Suomea?

"Do you speak Finnish?" This guide will help you to say the basic words and phrases in Finnish.

DATE & TIME

Monday/Tuesday	Maanantai/Tiistai
Wednesday/Thursday	Keskiviikko/Torstai
Friday/Saturday	Perjantai/Lauantai
Sunday/working day	Sunnuntai/arkipäivä
holiday	pyhäpäivä
today/tomorrow/yesterday	tänään/huomenna/eilen
hour/minute	tunti/minuutti
day/night/week/month/year	päivä/yö/viikko/kuukausi/vuosi
What time is it?	Paljonko kello on? Mitä kello on?
It's three o'clock	Kello on kolme
It's half past three	Kello on puoli neljä
a quarter to four	Kello on varttia vaille neljä
a quarter past four	Kello on varttia yli neljä

TRAVEL

open/closed	auki/suljettu
entrance	sisäänkäynti/sisäänajo
exit	uloskäynti/ulos(ajo)
departure/	lähtevät (junat)/lähtevät/
arrival	saapuvat
toilets women/men	WC (vessa)/Naiset/Miehet
Where is ...?/Where are ...?	Missä on ...?/Missä ovat ...?
left/right	vasemmalla/oikealla
straight ahead/back	suoraan eteenpäin/takaisin
close/far	lähellä/kaukana
bus/tram/	linja-auto (bussi)/raitiovaunu/
taxi/cab	taksi
parking lot/parking garage	pysäköintialue/pysäköintitalo
street map/map	kaupungin kartta/kartta
train station/harbour	rautatieasema/satama
airport	lentoasema
timetable/ticket	aikataulu/matkalippu
single/return	vain meno-(lippu)/menopaluu(matka)
train / track/platform	juna/raide
I would like to rent ...	Haluaisin vuokrata ...
a car/a bicycle/a boat	auto/polkupyörä/vene
petrol / gas station	huoltoasema
petrol/gas / diesel	bensiini/diesel
breakdown/repair shop	Autossani on vika/(auto)korjamo

FOOD & DRINK

The menu, please	Saisinko ruokalistan, toisitteko ruokalistan
Could I please have ...?	Saisinko ...
bottle/carafe/glass	pullo/kannu(ruukku)/lasi
a knife/a fork/a spoon	veitsi/haarukka/lusikka
salt/pepper/sugar	suola/pippuri/sokeri
vinegar/oil	etikka/öljy
milk/cream/lemon	maito/kerma/sitruuna
with/without ice/sparkling	jäillä/ilman jäitä/hiilihappo
vegetarian/allergy	kasvissyöjä/allergia
May I have the bill, please?	Lasku, olkaa hyvää
bill/receipt	lasku/kuitti
tip	juomaraha

SHOPPING

Where can I find...?	Missä on ...?
I'd like .../I'm looking for ...	Haluaisin .../etsin ...
pharmacy	apteekki
baker/market/market hall	leipomo/(kauppa)tori/kauppahalli
shopping centre/department store	ostoskeskus/tavaratalo
supermarket/kiosk	supermarket/kioski
100 grammes/1 kilo	sataa grammaa/kilo
expensive/cheap/price	kallis/halpa/hinta
more/less	enemmän/vähemmän
organically grown	luomu ...

ACCOMMODATION

I have booked a room	Olen varannut huoneen.
Do you have any ... left?	Onko teillä vielä ...
single (double) room	yhden- (kahden-)hengen huone
breakfast/half board	aamiainen/puolihoito
full board (American plan)	täysihoito
at the lakefront	järvelle
shower/sit-down bath	suihku/kylpyhuone
balcony/terrace	parveke/terassi
key/room card	avain/huonekortti
luggage/suitcase/bag	matkatavarat/matkalaukku/kassi, laukku

BANKS, MONEY & CREDIT CARDS

bank/ATM	pankki/pankkiautomaatti
pin code	salasana

cash/credit card	käteinen/ec-kortti/luottokortti
bill/coin	seteli/kolikko
change	vaihtoraha

HEALTH

doctor/dentist/paediatrician	lääkäri/hammaslääkäri/lastenlääkäri
hospital/emergency clinic	sairaala/päivystys, ensiapu
fever/pain	kuume/kipu, särky
diarrhoea/nausea	ripuli/pahoinvointi
inflamed/injured	tulehtunut/loukkaantunut
plaster/bandage	laastari/side
ointment/cream	voide/ihovoide
pain reliever/tablet	särkylääke/tabletti

POST, TELECOMMUNICATIONS & MEDIA

stamp/letter/postcard	postimerkki/kirje/ postikortti
I need a landline phone card/ I'm looking for a prepaid card for my mobile	tarvitsen puhelinkortin lankapuhelimeen/ Etsin prepaidkorttia kännykkääni
Do I need to dial a special code?	Tarvitsenko erikoista suuntanumeroa?
socket/adapter/charger	pistorasia/sovitin, adapteri/laturi
computer/battery/rechargeable battery	tietokone/paristo/akku
at sign (@)	miukumauku, ät
internet address (URL)	internet-osoite
e-mail address	sähköpostiosoite
internet connection/wifi	internet-yhteys/wlan
e-mail/file/print	sähköposti/tiedosto/tulostaa

NUMBERS

0	nolla	14	neljätoista
1	yksi	15	viisitoista
2	kaksi	16	kuusitoista
3	kolme	17	seitsemäntoista
4	neljä	18	kahdeksantoista
5	viisi	19	yhdeksäntoista
6	kuusi	20	kaksikymmentä
7	seitsemän	50	viisikymmentä
8	kahdeksan	100	sata
9	yhdeksän	101	satayksi
10	kymmenen	200	kaksisataa
11	yksitoista	1000	tuhat
12	kaksitoista	½	puoli
13	kolmetoista	¼	neljäsosa, neljännes

NOTES

ROAD ATLAS

The green line ▬▬▬ indicates the Trips & tours (p. 94–99)
The blue line ▬▬▬ indicates the Perfect route (p. 30–31)

All tours are also marked on the pull-out map

Photo: Rowing boat on Lake Saimaa

Exploring Finland

The map on the back cover shows how the area has been sub-divided

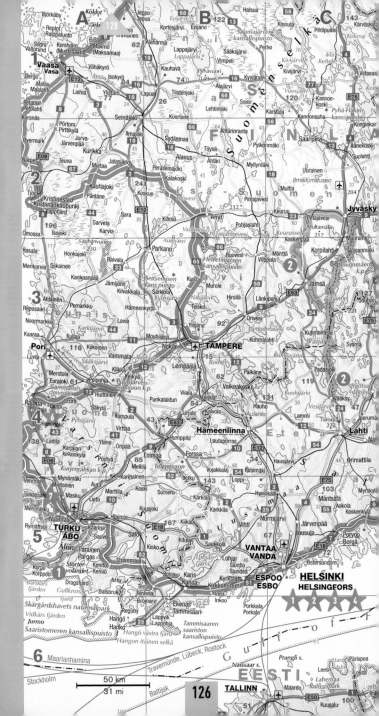

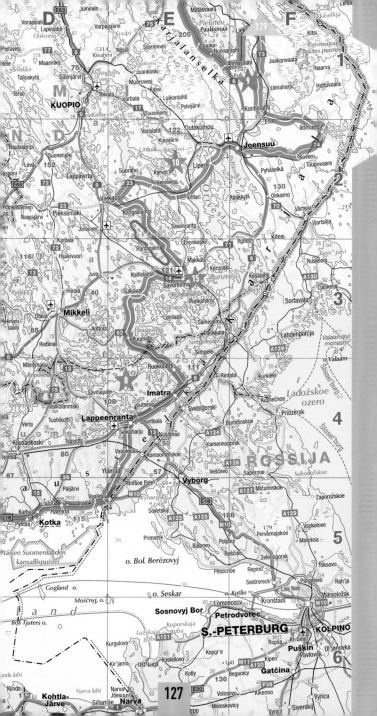

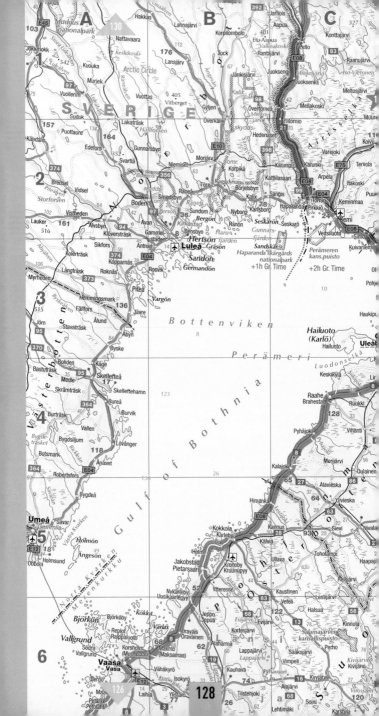

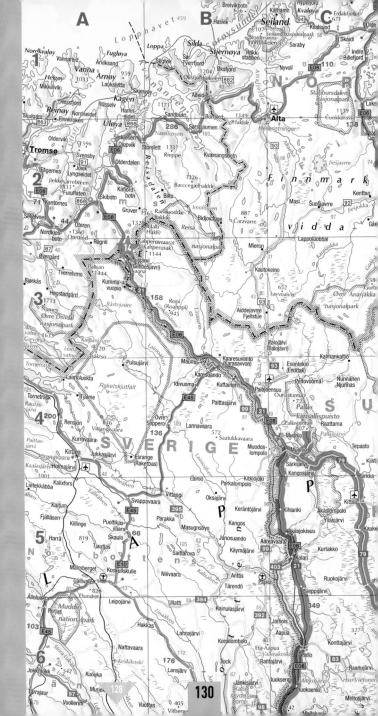

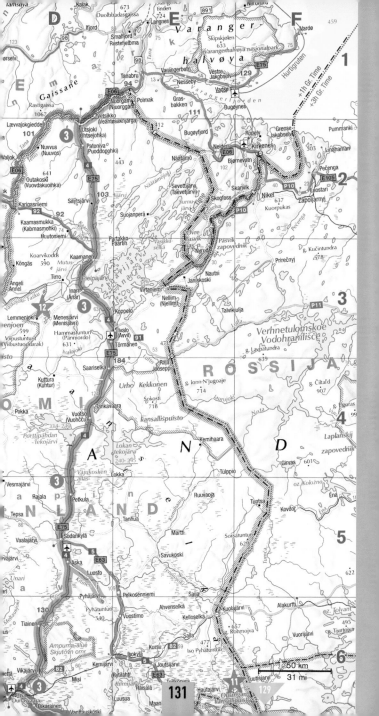

KEY TO ROAD ATLAS

Highway, multilane divided road - under construction Autobahn, mehrspurige Straße - in Bau		Autoroute, route à plusieurs voies - en construction Autosnelweg, weg met meer rijstroken - in aanleg
Trunk road - under construction Fernverkehrsstraße - in Bau		Route à grande circulation - en construction Weg voor interlokaal verkeer - in aanleg
Principal highway Hauptstraße		Route principale Hoofdweg
Secondary road Nebenstraße		Route secondaire Overige verharde wegen
Practicable road, track Fahrweg, Piste		Chemin carrossable, piste Weg, piste
Road numbering Straßennummerierung	E20 11 70 26	Numérotage des routes Wegnummering
Distances in kilometres Entfernungen in Kilometer	259 130 129	Distances en kilomètres Afstand in kilometers
Height in metres - Pass Höhe in Meter - Pass	1365	Altitude en mètres - Col Hoogte in meters - Pas
Railway - Railway ferry Eisenbahn - Eisenbahnfähre		Chemin de fer - Ferry-boat Spoorweg - Spoorpont
Car ferry - Shipping route Autofähre - Schifffahrtslinie		Bac autos - Ligne maritime Autoveer - Scheepvaartlijn
Major international airport - Airport Wichtiger internationaler Flughafen - Flughafen	✈ ✈	Aéroport importante international - Aéroport Belangrijke internationale luchthaven - Luchthaven
International boundary - Province boundary Internationale Grenze - Provinzgrenze		Frontière internationale - Limite de Province Internationale grens - Provinciale grens
Undefined boundary Unbestimmte Grenze		Frontière d'Etat non définie Rijksgrens onbepaalt
Time zone boundary Zeitzonengrenze	-4h Greenwich Time -3h Greenwich Time	Limite de fuseau horaire Tijdzone-grens
National capital Hauptstadt eines souveränen Staates	**HELSINKI**	Capitale nationale Hoofdstad van een soevereine staat
Federal capital Hauptstadt eines Bundesstaates	**Turku**	Capitale d'un état fédéral Hoofdstad van een deelstat
Restricted area Sperrgebiet		Zone interdite Verboden gebied
National park Nationalpark		Parc national Nationaal park
Ancient monument Antikes Baudenkmal	∴	Monuments antiques Antiek monument
Interesting cultural monument Sehenswertes Kulturdenkmal	∗ *Chambord*	Monument culturel intéressant Bezienswaardig cultuurmonument
Interesting natural monument Sehenswertes Naturdenkmal	∗ *Gorges du Tarn*	Monument naturel intéressant Bezienswaardig natuurmonument
Well Brunnen		Puits Bron
Trips & tours Ausflüge & Touren		Excursions & tours Uitstapjes & tours

INDEX

This index lists all places and sights featured in this guide. Numbers in bold indicate a main entry.